SEEKING

74 Key Findings to
Raise Your Energy,
Sidestep your Self-Doubts, and
Align with Your Life's Work

JJ DiGeronimo

ISBN Paperback: 979-8-9856897-6-1
ISBN Hardcover: 979-8-9856897-7-8
ISBN Electronic: 979-8-9856897-5-4

Library of Congress Control Number: 2022917572

Editors:
Heidi Bright, MDiv: HeidiBright.com
Zora Alexandra Knauf: ZoraAlexandraKnauf@gmail.com

Cover Design: Nicole Daberkow: NicoleDaberkow.com

Publishing Consultant: PRESStinely: PRESStinely.com

Author Photo: DawnKaye Photography, LLC, DawnKayePhoto.com

Portions of this book are works of nonfiction. Certain names and identifying characteristics have been changed.

Printed in the United States of America.

Together We Seek Publishing

Website: JJDiGeronimo.com
Community: TogetherWeSeek.Online
Download Book Questions: JJDiGeronimo.com/YourSeeking

Let's Connect on Social: @JJDiGeronimo

Thank you to all the beautiful souls, lessons, and experiences that brought me right here, right now.

I'm especially grateful for my family, who support me and my work, and for all the people who had a special role in making this come to life.

Let Our Light Shine

CONTENTS

PREFACE

When nudged by the Universe to write this book, my initial response was *I'm not ready.* That was followed with *I still have more to learn.* Yet after each women's event where I was invited to present, I would share some of these insights and exercises, and the noticeable interest was reassuring, validating that women were ready to talk more about their self-doubts and fears. They were ready to be more vulnerable and more vocal about what they needed and what they desired. I saw this engagement as permission to share my journey, even if it expanded beyond career books, skill assessments, and emotional intelligence tests.

The conversations and experiences in these pages go beyond the professional and corporate strategies I have previously shared with my readers and communities. So, if you are familiar with my work, you may initially be surprised, yet I have found that I needed to go beyond the traditional methods to understand my internal barriers and gain new levels of insight.

When I questioned many of my life circumstances, I turned to books, podcasts, alternative practices, and non-conventional healers. These gave me access to the wisdom of my Soul. Ancient practices unleashed my bound-up energy so it could serve my higher purpose. In the pages ahead, I will share these self-discoveries as tools to help illuminate your path.

I am now certain that there is more to our stories, existences, and even our work than we originally perceive. It is a bit scary, yet I believe that now is the time for more of our gifts and wisdom to emerge so we can empower each other at work and in life.

At first I questioned myself and felt nervous about sharing this, yet I believe that my journey—which includes many moments of feeling uncertain, alone, defeated, and depleted—can inspire your journey. And maybe you will use these strategies to inspire others on their journeys, as we are here on this planet to help each other find and align with more love and light.

We are all part of an unconditional loving flow of energy that you can tap into anytime to illuminate your gifts, connections, and life's work. This energy can even help you remember why you chose to be on this planet right now.

I am looking forward to being with you here, now, even if this is all new to you or I am sharing words that do not resonate with you yet. Trust that you are here for a reason. There are nuggets ahead that will help you raise your energy and align with your life's work.

INTRODUCTION

If you are tired of chasing standards that are imposed on you by others; if you are drowning in to-do lists that deplete your energy and maybe even your impact; if you are swimming in negative thoughts and self-talk; or if you are simply seeking more meaning…you are not alone!

I, too, felt an internal tug for something more. I was unsettled for years. In hindsight, I now recognize it was my heart that was pulling me so fiercely to pursue more meaning beyond my day job and roles at home.

At first, I pushed the feeling away and tried to convince myself that I was FINE. Yet my inner turmoil did not quit! It pushed me to seek new conversations, new classes, and new books. Throughout this book I will refer to this concept of *seeking*—pursuing personal fulfillment off the side of my desk; away from my job. Not everything I discovered was aligned with and relevant to what my heart wanted, but throughout my seeking, I found new areas of excitement and new sources of energy, which I call fuel stations. These new activities energized my inner self and my Soul. This provided reprieve and balance as my fatigued mind continued to chase external metrics such as work milestones, titles, and accolades.

As I said, you are not alone. Through my journey, I discovered that many women I meet are experiencing some level of misalignment because they are working on projects or are tolerating relationships that are draining their good energy and dimming their lights, preventing them from unleashing their life's work.

Many people assume that when you are "successful" or when you get to a certain level at work or in life, you will experience bliss or joy. Well, this did not happen for me. Sure, I had moments of joy, but I also had many hours, even days on end, of feeling less than full. Little did I know, I had a sprouting purpose from within that was not satisfied by my external striving and goals. My internal guide, my Soul, was seeking alignment with my true life's work.

In the pages ahead, I give you glimpses of my story, as well as the stories of other women, for the purpose of helping you on your own path. You will discover the common obstacles that hinder our progress in finding our life's work and what you can do to overcome these obstacles.

I have also included reflection questions and exercises developed from the insights I gleaned from my seeking. I used and still use these guiding questions as a way to dig deep into myself, release my guilt, and tap into more of my inner knowing. Through this continuous attention and reflection, I have found far more joy, alignment, and fulfillment than any external accomplishment has ever provided. You can download the questions with an email at https://jjdigeronimo. com/yourseeking.

With so many instrumental lessons along my path, I have included a key finding at the end of each chapter, as well as key findings interspersed throughout the text if they arose for me during a particular lesson or experience. Along with using this book as a tool, you might find it helpful to keep track of your thoughts, answers, ideas, questions, and your own key findings in a notebook.

Many of us know we have a bigger purpose than the one we are living. My hope is that by the end of this book, you will feel empowered to tap into your inner wisdom by listening to your whispers, recognizing the energy that depletes you, and working on releasing your stories.

In this book, you will find…

- Ideas for how to explore your desires,
- Strategies for sorting out your options,
- Questions for discovering what obstacles may be holding you back, and
- Suggestions to help you energize your journey.

Your situations have brought you right here to these pages, which may…

- Awaken your inner knowing,
- Fuel your unique light,
- Expand your existing sphere, and
- Illuminate your path.

There is an abundance of support available to you as you discover opportunities to reconnect with your inner light. Beyond these pages, you can join me and women like you in an online community, www.TogetherWeSeek.Online, where we share, learn, and empower each other. You also can explore one of my retreats or gatherings for personal connections with other seekers like you.

By making time to dive into these pages, you are showing the Universe that you are ready for the next step, next chapter, next situation, next version, next anything that life is ready to bring your way.

You may be called to jump around the chapters or go straight through the book. Like life, it is your adventure, so I encourage you to pay attention to how you feel, what is coming up for you, and what you are trying to avoid. All these choices carry messages for you about where you are right now and why.

Upon reading this book, you will understand the underpinnings of your urge to seek. This seeking, from the inside out, offers suggestions for shifts in schedules, thoughts, and desires. How much or how little you decide to act on these suggestions at any given time is also up to you.

As you work through this book, be sure you are open to a shift, even a small one. Life does not often provide safe opportunities for being vulnerable. Your willingness to open the door to your inner world can feel risky, yet this book is a safe place where you can explore what is happening with your feelings, emotions, stories, and level of doubt or confidence in yourself. All of these are pieces that drive your decisions and external actions.

Not everyone makes it to this part of her or his life's journey, as it is beyond what many feel comfortable exploring, sharing, or discussing. This next level of self-awareness is full of adventures, and it is almost inevitable that you will question your current state of existence, alignment, and joy.

If you are lucky enough to be asking yourself, "What is this all for?", or "Now what?", or "Is there more?", then you are ready to embark on your next step of self-discovery.

Your internal exploration and external seeking can unveil the next level of your life's work. This is an exciting time in which you are ready to cross over from where you have been to where you are going! I am thrilled to be embarking on this together, in a space where you can work to shift your focus and frequency.

Let's explore ways to illuminate your path ahead, from the inside out!

Key Finding #1

If you are here, you have already started your next level of awakening.

QUIZ: IS THIS BOOK FOR YOU?

As of today, check all that apply:

- ☐ I have many accomplishments
- ☐ I wish I had more accomplishments
- ☐ I often take on more than I should
- ☐ I know there is more to me that I want to explore
- ☐ Finding time for myself is not always easy
- ☐ I wish I felt more confident
- ☐ I want a tribe of people who also are seeking
- ☐ I yearn for real conversation and connection
- ☐ I am yearning for more but I am unsure how to manifest it
- ☐ I need to take the time to heal my past
- ☐ I am interested in exploring different things, off the side of my desk
- ☐ I would like to go to retreats or on a solo trip
- ☐ I know I have untapped talents
- ☐ I am interested in living with less fear
- ☐ I believe I am at a crossroads
- ☐ I am ready to seek

If you resonated with many of these, you are likely ready for a shift—and you may even be experiencing some of these:

- Drowning in your to-do list
- Chasing external metrics to define self-worth
- Swimming in negative thoughts and self-talk
- Questioning your purpose
- Seeking more alignment or meaning
- Trying to figure out how life fits together

Take a picture of your checkboxes above. Mark it as a favorite photo so you can easily find it to reference the date. If you are feeling excited or bold, feel free to share the photo with me on Instagram @JJDiGeronimo so I can send some great energy your way as you embark on this new chapter in your life. Then, read on, as the pages ahead are filled with some of the strategies I used after recognizing that I, too, checked many of the boxes above and was ready to seek.

Key Finding #2

It is important to document your starting point.

Your Soul is yearning for you to reach new
heights of awareness.

Trust that you are being guided to seek your
next level of awakening.

Be curious, embrace what comes forward for you,
and be ready to raise your frequency.

PART I

STEPPING INTO THE WHISPERS

CHAPTER 1

THE TURMOIL WITHIN MY YESES

I had hit a wall from overproducing, over-delivering, and over-committing. Quite frankly, I was over it, questioning all aspects of my life.

I, like many women, left little time for myself. I was busy working, taking care of family, and helping everyone and everything else that came my way. I cut myself out of my schedule too often, leaving myself depleted and, at times, very unhealthy.

Even after years of leadership training, I did not know where to start or how to get the heck out of my own way. I had been beating myself up for years—from the demands I put on myself, to the many times I said "yes" when I should have said "no." I was my worst enemy and I was ready for a shift.

I tried drinking more wine, sabotaging my marriage, and even considered driving away and never coming back. Luckily, I did not follow through on any of those wishes, as I later learned that those sabotaging thoughts were reflecting how unsettled I felt on the inside.

This undermining energy had been building up for years, but I had just continued to do what I did best—pushing through my to-do list with my head down. The actions that usually distracted me from my internal whispers had me questioning all aspects of my life, landing me in a therapist's office while wishing for a hospital bed. I'd had enough, and I was ready to check out.

I could have pointed outward and blamed many other people, yet my vast self-help book collection would attest that I was wiser. I knew there was no other way to point the blame than to turn that finger inward. I was fully aware that my current state started and ended with me. I just did not know how to get untangled from all my "yeses" and expectations that I and others had thrown my way. I needed a good, old-fashioned reboot.

I now recognize that feeling depleted and, at times, depressed was the result of striving outward. It was not until I gave enough attention to the internal tug of my Soul that I realized that I had to make a conscious shift.

Here is something I captured while taking a walk in 2017, which I believe encapsulates the transition that was happening inside.

Sometimes I feel so lost in my own life.

I feel that I'm not completely connected to the reason I am here.

I feel like I'm missing a connection bigger than myself.

When I look around, I see so much beauty in God's creations, but I often cannot feel that energy running through me.

I desire to feel how I am part of this bigger Universal energy that flows through all living creatures.

I struggle with my true purpose.

I often feel that it's not exactly right and I'm not exactly sure why.

As I walk along my path, a feather appears.

Feathers are an indication for me that I'm not alone and that God's guidance and spiritual wisdom are all around me.

I listen, watch, and feel for a glimmer of connection beyond where I am right now.

I feel emptier more than I want to admit.

And I'm not sure why.

I have so many things around me, so many friendships, and so much love, yet my Soul is reaching out of my chest to connect with something bigger than myself.

My walk in nature is a journey as I watch, look, connect, and feel how the wind touches my face and my feet touch the ground.

My heart feels the animals, and I notice how the smell of the earth travels through my nose.

Where is the message?

Is there a message, or is this a natural way for me to just relax and be in nature?

What am I searching for?

What have I been doing, visiting all these energy and spiritual practitioners?

I have been cleaning my vessel, aligning with my light source, and finding ways to do my work.

I should be celebrating the fact that I have the ability, support, and connection to channel my work through me to you.

But sometimes, I get sad, depressed, and disconnected.

Sharing my journey gives me inspiration and appreciation.

We need each other, as we're doing this together, even though we may have not yet met.

This is why we are connecting here, because what society has laid out does not align with women's Souls.

So I'll take you on a journey of where I've been, what I'm doing, and what I'm learning, and I hope you will do what you need for your journey.

We are part of the same energy, the same light, and the same love.

My shift from outward to inward occurred after the seeking had begun. As I learned to look inward more often for recognition, power, and security, the next level of my life's work emerged.

Key Finding #3

Your journey is created just for you, and even if you feel lost or misaligned, this thing called life is happening for you and not to you.

CHAPTER 2

THE SHIFT IS HAPPENING

Women who cross my path are often searching. Sometimes they know what they are searching for, yet many are sitting with doubts about their inner voices, their work, and their lives.

How you landed inside these pages could be a mystery or a direct line. In either case, now is the perfect time to explore your thoughts and your stories, as these are likely what have defined your life up to this point.

Before we jump inside, it is essential to note that, as women, we have not been able to show up at work with all our tools and unique talents. The existing societal matrix apparent in most corporate structures is primarily designed by masculine energies.

There is harmony when masculine and feminine energy work together and each of us have both energies. Masculine energy is often categorized as getting, doing, and defining, whereas feminine energy is more often associated with knowing, connecting, and being. Either of these energies could be more or less pronounced in some people or even some situations. With millions of search results on the differences, you could research this for hours, but my point here is too much of either energy makes things lopsided.

Many of these cultures and environments have required us to minimize our feminine energy and intuition to succeed. To adapt, we have tried to be more like men. To fit in, we had to limit ourselves to only half of our wisdom and energy to produce, create, and deliver. Even with great results, many of us still feel unfilled and even like outsiders.

The good news is you are on this planet during a time of a global energetic shift. On December 21, 2012, the Mayan calendar ended, and many people view this event as the beginning of a new cycle that involves the balancing of feminine and masculine energies of this planet.

This new universal cycle opened the gateway, awakening women who are interested and ready to reconnect with themselves, rediscover their unique gifts, and realign their actions with the shifting energetic patterns of our planet.

As if to help signal this shift, we are seeing an upswing in activities that address inequities at work. Some say it is not enough, but I think we can all agree there is a groundswell emerging through a series of events, including the COVID-19 pandemic, the #MeToo movement, reproductive choices, labor shortages, and the uncertainties around the world.

Combine this with my own observation: Women are questioning their experiences and goals while searching for more meaning within their current choices. With emerging levels of burnout and depression, it is no surprise people are searching for new, more enlightening waves of energy.

It is time for us to step into the universal shift that started in 2012. Many of us have been sitting on the perimeters, only thinking about stepping up, jumping in, signing up, speaking up, or starting something new. Now more than ever, this planet needs us to join in at more tables to help make more decisions. The calling is upon us now to make the time to investigate our internal nudges, seek new areas of wisdom, and believe in what we have to share with the world. We need to believe in ourselves, step into our light, and use our gifts to balance the masculine and feminine energies.

Our work, whether big or small, will be part of the universal energy that will harmonize masculine and feminine energies. To do this, we have to start within. We will need to:

- Understand our stories
- Be mindful of our fears
- Let go of what is no longer serving us
- Create space for awareness and love
- Rediscover our gifts, and
- Realign our actions with our true callings.

For many of us, this will start in small ways, off the sides of our desks, counters, and tablets, yet collectively, universal energy will emerge to support us as we shift our planet into more balance and harmony.

Now is the time to step into our light, use our gifts, and believe in our work. This requires us, as women, to dust off our innate talents, invest in ourselves and each other, and align with what we know is true.

Key Finding #4

Many women inherently know they have a bigger calling that starts from within.

Let me assure you
Everything you have experienced up to this point
was perfectly orchestrated to get you here, right now.

And, even if things do not make sense

Everything has its place in your evolution and growth.

You can choose to embrace and learn
from your experiences
or
deflect and deny them
yet
the lessons will appear
and
your experiences will continue.

This is
Your Experience,
Your Life,
Your Journey.

CHAPTER 3

GIVING YOURSELF PERMISSION

It took me years to acknowledge that this was me: a woman who was wrestling with her past and camouflaging her fears. My most common disguises were perfectionism and workaholism, which showed up as over-delivering and over-committing. I was mostly unsettled. I yearned for more self-love, moments of joy, and purposeful interactions, but I was lost in my schedule with little time to seek.

Yes, the titles, trips, salary, car, and suburban life were nice, but the laughter and fulfillment were brief because there was always more to get done. I defined myself by my salary and title. It was sad but true that I did not realize I had such a profound lack of self-worth.

And when I leaped into entrepreneurship with the purpose of making a more significant difference, I found myself feeling even more alone. I had no external self-worth metrics to hold onto, which left me embarrassed and at times depressed.

Looking back, I find it ironic that I thought I was ready to help others when, in reality, I first needed to help myself.

During my initial efforts to seek my truth, I realized I was not alone. Many women are unsure and unsettled. Many are struggling with self-worth issues and are afraid to step out in new ways. I often hear women say, "I can do more," yet this phrase is quickly teamed with "I am not enough" or "I am not ready."

Questions to ask:

Do you feel unsettled or find yourself yearning for more?

_____

_____

Are you questioning your purpose or life's work?

_____

_____

Do you question your thoughts or feelings?

_____

_____

How does your title or salary define your worth? Or your car, purse, trips, or zip code?

_____

_____

You may initially say, "No, they don't," but think about what life would be like without the things we use as tools to tell people who we are. Who would you be and what worth do you think you would lean on without material things or titles?

_____

_____

Are you overworked or burned out?

_____

_____

Are you finding yourself sad and disengaged?

_____

_____

How have you been striving and reaching?

_____

_____

Do you create the joy you expected?

_____

_____

Do you still find yourself striving to feed your inner desire to achieve so you can prove you can do it?

_____

_____

Are you questioning your choices?

_____

_____

It seems that our current society is accomplishment driven, using a hierarchical structure that many of us must participate in if we choose to work outside the home. The required deliverables, culture, and structure easily camouflage, pass over, or derail our inherent feminine knowing and our inner wisdom, forcing us to leave some of our gifts, which we are here to share, at the door.

This loss or separation of skills creates a lopsided approach to life on Earth, with a promise of self-fulfillment that never really manifests.

The calling upon us now is to step into our knowing and uncover those gifts that will help balance the masculine and feminine energies. This requires us to make the time to dust off our innate talents, invest in ourselves, and align with what we know is true. We must do this both independently and together. I know there are some Soul memories that block women from having fully transparent and dependable relationships. These are experiences and stories that our Souls recall. We have carried this energy here with us, and through our self-exploration and alignment, we can mend those strands.

By healing, we are empowered to rebuild our trust in each other. This will happen in two steps. First, we must work to accept ourselves from the inside out. This work will help us uncover space for more love and light. Then, together, we will unite our lights and self-acceptance to elevate our frequencies and the frequency of the planet.

If you are a woman seeking deeper connections, more moments of joy, more fulfilling activities, and more meaningful work, this is no accident. Your inner self knows there is more to your work here on Earth. Women from all walks of life are seeking realignment, even if their physical state is unaware of this desire. I know this because I regularly encounter women who are awakening to energies, desires, and new levels of connection; women who know there is more to their lives than what they are experiencing today.

Regardless of your current state, recognize the messages you are receiving that provide insight into your fears and self-doubts, which tend to hold many of us back, while giving yourself permission to make your desires a reality.

Key Finding #5
There are no mistakes in your experiences and yearning.

CHAPTER 4

ADJUSTING YOUR FREQUENCY

Seeking my truth from the inside out was not easy, and I had many pit stops and winding roads, but I did not see any other option.

My desire for a shift motivated me to dig through my stories, work to remove unresolved issues and even pain, realign my energy with my deeper desires, and let go of what was no longer serving me.

How are you feeling right now?

- Excited
- Nervous
- Concerned
- Ready
- Reluctant
- Connected
- Intimidated
- Worried
- Enthusiastic

Take a few minutes to expand on how you are feeling:

_____

_____

It is not easy to make a shift or even to make time for some new information. Yet, I have learned that to step into my next level of work and impact, I often have to check and align my energy or frequency.

Your energetic self is likely attracted to the energy or frequency of this message, whether or not you fully understand why. A frequency is a wave of energy. Consider, for a moment, the radio in your car. FM radio stands for frequency modulation, and each station sends out signals attuned to specific frequencies. Just as you are drawn to specific radio stations, the vibrational frequency that you hold, maintain, or nurture right now is drawing to you the frequency of the messages and tools inside this book.

Key Finding #6

Your Soul knows the lessons it came to learn.

Note: There is no pressure to do, say, or be anything that does not feel comfortable. Know that there is nothing ahead that is scary or dangerous. This work is surrounded by love and acceptance that aligns with a higher or illuminated energy, which I call God, but refer to it as you see fit. This high energy is beyond me and connects all of us in a band or frequency of light and love.

Some of our human learnings and religious practices discourage us from tapping into this love and light on our own, but I encourage you to allow your heart to find its way. Note also that your ego—the energy that comes with your human body that likes to be in control and act as a protector—might trigger fears. Therefore, be sure you are aware of where your desires are coming from—your heart or your head.

Before we move forward, I want to take a minute to bring your attention to the appendices, located at the end of this book, where I have listed many of the people, services, products, and conversations I have put to good use along the way. I would also like to explain a few terms I will be using in this book that relate to energy.

- **Frequency:** The sum of your energy resulting from your awareness, connection, and acceptance you have with yourself and the world around you. Many have identified frequency ranges with certain feelings, experiences, and emotions. You can alter your frequency at any time, taking it up or down, which affects whether you are feeling good or bad. Your frequency often shifts based on how you perceive your life experiences.

- **Energy Practices:** Experiences, exercises, or activities that focus on the flow or frequency inside and around you.

- **Energy Practitioners:** People who facilitate the movement of energy inside or around you. They may or may not use healing methods, but they often can help you discover, pinpoint, or experience energy in a new way.

- **Ancient Practices:** Experiences, exercises, or activities that have been used for hundreds of years to move energy, shift frequencies, align with Mother Nature, give thanks, pray, recognize the season, work with the Universal flow, or facilitate healing.

- **Sphere of Influence:** The people you attract and align with at any one time. They often connect with your frequency and may impact your goals.

- **Lightworkers:** People dedicated to sharing their gifts to help others create room for more love and light by using awareness, tools, insights, lessons, and gifts.

If you are here with me now, it is time for you to prioritize your inner knowing, which will lead you to a higher level of energy. Let's spend time understanding what may be holding you back. Finding the levers to pull those obstacles aside will move you beyond where you are now to increase your sphere of light and alignment.

Key Finding #7

Up-leveling into the frequency of the Universal light takes time, acceptance, and side-stepping the ego so you can find peace and love within yourself first.

CHAPTER 5

OVERCOMMITTED YET YEARNING FOR MORE

I have noticed an alarming level of annoyance, dissatisfaction, and exhaustion among women. And yet, when I talk with women at events or gatherings, most share that they desire more influence or impact. Many say they still have more to do, create, be, and say. These desires are exactly why we are here right now.

Let me ask you:

- Are you still yearning for more levels of influence?
- Do you feel like you have more things to do and share?
- Are you noticing an inner desire to seek?

However, even with these desires and aspirations, many of us have too much on our plates. By the time we reach the end of each day, many of us are left with little time to raise our frequency and align with the next stage of our life's work. Many of us doubt our inner whispers and are unsure how to shift. Feeling defeated or deflated, we allow ourselves to be distracted by our insecurities, relationships, and situations.

I know this all too well. For decades I let my fears drive my schedule, swimming in the "I'm too busy" mantra that would feed my ego and starve my Soul. I squeezed alone time, personal appointments, and enriching activities out of my schedule, then praised myself for being productive, knowing that I was robbing myself of what I really needed.

How do you feel about your current commitments? (Satisfied, Overwhelmed, Indifferent, etc.)

_____

_____

How can you group the commitments in your week? (Work, Family, Community, etc.)

_____

_____

Where do you experience joy and fulfillment within your week?

_____

_____

What have you set aside that you wish you had more time for each week?

_____

_____

Even when I knew I needed to seek and shift, I did not begin until other aspects of my life were derailed. It took some stops and starts, and many of the activities and initiatives began off the side of my desk.

Key Finding #8

If your schedule is demanding and you still don't feel fulfilled, seeking is a great place to start.

CHAPTER 6

SUMMONED TO SEEK

For years my self-worth was defined by a salary and title, but honestly, I did not know any better. I was encouraged to strive, from an early age, and was praised for doing so.

As each milestone appeared, I moved further away from what I call my inner compass, which holds my universal knowing and my connection to a more significant "why."

Yet despite the outward rewards and successes that come with a technology career in Silicon Valley, I was summoned to seek. It started as a feeling that would appear every now and then, more than a decade and a half ago, and eventually grew into an undeniable sense of disconnection.

I found myself yearning for more, even though I was meeting and exceeding my professional goals. The joy I had expected at this stage of my career did not appear, outside of a few moments here and there, and my to-dos at work and at home were never-ending.

I was unsure what to do. After many long days and nights, I fell into new levels of self-doubt and loneliness that pushed me to question almost all aspects of my life. Eager to get out of my own way, and get out for some wine with women, I started bringing women together locally.

At times I thought I was crazy to add more to my to-dos, but I needed meaningful connections, more empathy for what I was juggling, and frankly, some guidance. I had few expectations beyond getting together with women who had similar experiences and roles in the technology field. Little did I know that these gatherings would be the basis for the next chapter of my life's work.

The initial insights gathered during these Tech Savvy Women meetups were the basis for my first book on working women with young children, which I titled *The Working Woman's GPS: When the Plan to Have It All Has Led You Astray.* The lessons I learned from these women, while we enjoyed light snacks and wine together, would eventually be shared with tens of thousands more and mark the beginning of my women-in-business journey. After continued seeking and learning, I eventually published my second book, *Accelerate Your Impact: Action-Based Strategies to Pave Your Professional Path,* a guide for women looking to advance in their careers.

Even after many evolutions, I continue to learn from my journey and from the journeys of women who cross my path. With firsthand experiences and stories collected from many women, I am meeting you here, now, to share the next level of wisdom I have gathered to elevate and empower your seeking.

Looking back, I think of everything that brought me to this moment: the fears, successes, disappointments, and celebrations. I encourage you to take some time to reflect on the highlights of your life—and the low moments, too, as I have found that the lower moments can act as a catalyst for momentum ahead.

We are not expected to have it all figured out at any time, especially when we first start something new. So think of the time you spend with me as a launching pad for what may be ahead. And remember, I am not encouraging any upheavals. Life is a series of small steps that create momentum over time.

Key Finding #9
Small steps can create sparks of light for what is ahead.

CHAPTER 7

YOUR TIME TO EXPLORE

Your seeking is all yours, and you can unpackage it like a gift, any way you see fit. At this point in your life and your journey, treat yourself to some time and space for recapturing your desires and nudges.

I want to explore: _____
_____

I feel more inspired to: _____
_____

I already do _____, and it inspires me:
_____
_____

I can make more time for these activities because they inspire me:
_____
_____

These thoughts or ideas have reappeared or come forward since I started this book:
_____
_____

As my Pilates teachers, Amanda, Abby, and Julie, remind me at various times, "It is your practice. There is no performance or recital at the end." I will add that you are on your stage right now, so go at your own pace, honor your heart, mind, and body, and align with your inner light, because this is your time and your life.

Key Finding #10

This is your journey. Make time for what inspires you.

CHAPTER 8

THE ILLUSION OF SUCCESS

After college graduation, I leaped into a full-time role as a consultant based in Atlanta, Georgia. I found the dynamics of corporate America incredible— the paychecks, the training, the travel, the projects, and the engagement with professionals of all ages.

It was more mentally stimulating than I could have imagined back in high school when I was gazing over my shoulder at business data projected onto the screen as I replenished the coffee stations and Danish pastries. This, along with the white tablecloths and well-dressed professionals, was the vision that left a lasting impression.

Thanks to my Aunt Sue, I worked my fair share of weddings and birthday parties as a country club waitress, but it was the business meetings I remembered the most. I promised myself that one day, I would create the opportunity to be sitting in a similar conference room. Little did I know that my self-proclaimed vision would materialize in less than a decade. I quickly found myself pursuing the corporate dreams of access, security, experiences, money, power, and recognition, which many could refer to as professional success.

I now realize that this chase is an oasis. It creates an illusion that comes with a sea of obligations and expectations each week, requiring trade-offs and conditioning us to over-strive for external metrics. These weeks turn into years that end up detaching us from our inner knowing, especially if we skip things that inspire us, which I refer to as our fuel stations.

It was not long before I found myself striving for this oasis of success, which drove me to rise early and go to bed late. My focus was defined by my schedule, relationships, and actions, and these unfolded into daily to-dos. I later came to realize that the path to professional success is rather predictable and often programmed into us at an early age.

As professionals, we experience a variety of highs and lows, regrets, and celebrations; some experience more of some and less of others. Many women have shared with me that it was the unexpected twists and turns in their careers and lives that led them to undeniable feelings or decisions:

- Loss of a parent or loved one.
- Separation or divorce.
- Bankruptcy.
- Children leaving the house or getting married.
- Unexpected life events.

These events or others can often act as catalysts, leaving us questioning our choices and goals.

What unexpected twists or turns have activated your seeking?

_____

_____

Women who cross my path are often seeking, and it usually happens after some type of life event.

 ### *Key Finding #11*

Our actions are based on beliefs, and those beliefs stem from feelings that were generated by the stories we tell ourselves. Our stories often keep our fears at the forefront and thereby impact our choices and path.

Through all the stories and journeys women have shared with me, there seems to be a common trade-off for success that often robbed them of enjoyment, family time, and fun. And many find themselves, just like me, taking out the activities that bring fulfillment so they can check another item off the to-do list to avoid the potential embarrassment or fear of not being good enough.

Have you stepped down your goals to invest in your family or other projects?

_____

_____

What do you wish you knew earlier in your life that would have benefited you now?

_____

_____

What brings you the most joy?

_____

_____

How often do you do things that inspire or fill you up?

_____

_____

If the end was near, what would you wish you had done more often?

_____

_____

What skills, gifts, or wisdom want more time in your schedule?

_____

_____

What warms your heart or feeds your Soul?

_____

_____

Early on in my career I found it difficult to answer these questions. My attention was focused on the oasis of success. I justified my sacrifices and believed that my schedule aligned with the "right" goals. I later realized that my focus was primarily motivated by stories I learned as a child, along with my fear of failure, which was deeply rooted in my ego.

As I look at these questions, I now realize that while I was working toward professional success, I was not present during most moments. Instead, I was often planning for the future or reflecting on the past. I worried about what I did or what was expected of me. I constantly questioned my actions and abilities. If I had addressed these questions years ago, my answers would have been token responses created by my ego and based on my desire to push away my fears. I later came to understand that I was not aligned with my inner light or all my gifts.

I wish I had invested in a career coach much earlier in my professional life. This could have helped me better understand who I was and what I was running toward. Questions I wish I had discussed were:

What does success look like for you?

_____

_____

How is your interpretation of success managing or driving your actions and decisions?

_____

_____

Are you sacrificing too much of what lights you up as you drive toward your professional milestones, or have you found ways to incorporate things you love along the way?

_____

_____

Many women have figured out how to do things off the sides of their desks that keep them centered, whole, and enlightened. From online classes to meditation to gardening to working from home, there are many things you can do to help you keep your light bright, your frequency high, and your heart full of joy.

As you think about how you answered the questions above, be honest as you now ask yourself:

- How do my answers make me feel?
- Am I answering from a place of thinking or of feeling?
- Do I know the difference?

When I was younger, I would have answered the questions the way I thought I "should." That fact indicated where my work needed to begin. I now recognize that much of what I was striving for on the outside was a direct reflection of how I was feeling on the inside.

The illusion of success, with its sea of obligations and expectations, requires trade-offs. It essentially conditions us to over-strive for external metrics and detaches us from our inner knowing. This often leaves us disconnected and drained.

The illusion of success has been used to justify sacrifices, lies, and actions that rob us of our time, enjoyment, alignment, relationships, and peace of mind. These beliefs stem from internal stories that keep our fears at the forefront and impact our choices and life paths. As we strive for success at work and home, we often overlook our innate talents and spiritual gifts because we are focused outward.

This disconnect can start to appear in thoughts, ideas, or insights. For some, it may occur without expectation or preparation, but for me, it began to sprout after I became a mom and a leader. Eager to be better at both, I started a women's group (2008), which led to my first book (2011), and then to a solo trip to Sedona (2013), during which I was looking for reassurance that my inner nudges and whispers were worth exploring.

Like many, I started chasing the oasis of success in my twenties, but over time, the fulfillment I expected never appeared. Little by little, I was introduced to new ways of thinking and feeling, and I gradually shifted my energy and decisions from my head to my heart. This shift created higher frequencies, yet it took years of practice to unleash a deeper knowing and awareness.

I am still unraveling stories, fears, doubts, and insecurities, yet I also know that part of my life's work is to share what I have learned to make your seeking easier and more accessible. To do this, I am learning to be more vulnerable and accepting of my flaws. Each piece is part of my story and, like you, they are part of who we are as the collective energy on this planet.

Key Finding #12

The illusion of success could have you shackled.

CHAPTER 9

THE "I SHOULDS" OF SUCCESS

The "I should" mindset tormented me for years, and from what I understand, I am not alone. Many women struggle with the many asks that come their way—often saying "Yes" even when the asks are too big, outside their scope, not a good use of their time, or not aligned with their desires or goals.

The *I should because* mindset includes thoughts such as:

- I should because they need me,
- I should because who else is going to do it,
- I should because they expect me to help,
- I should because I want them to like me, or
- I should because I can.

Are you living your life from a place of "I should"? If so, you are not alone. The "I should" mindset continues to burden so many women. I will go even further and say that when you are working on others' goals, you are interfering with the energy that is trying to flow your way.

The hard truth is:

- Every time you say "Yes" to help another, you are taking a piece or chunk of your time that you could be dedicating to activities that could align with some of your passion projects and even eventually your life's work.

- You may love to help, but are you doing it for the right reasons, or are you doing it because you fear what will happen if you do not say "Yes"?
- Many of us have been taught from an early age to be helpful, be kind, smile, be nice, and be gracious. Many of us go beyond what is needed to be sure others like and accept us.

How does this land for you? Where are you on the *I should* spectrum?

_____

_____

The exercise below can be a one-time activity, or you can check your *I shoulds* each week to assess how many things land in your calendar. I often run through this list, and it amazes me how often I give away my time. Instead, I should be saving to invest in my passion projects, my gifts, and my aspirations.

What on your calendar this week or month applies?

- "I should be _____ "
- "I should do _____ "
- "I should go _____ "
- "I should help _____ "
- "I should call _____ "
- "I should take _____ "
- "I should drive _____ "
- "I should stay _____ "
- "I should make _____ "
- "I should manage _____ "
- "I should lead _____ "
- "I should stop _____ "
- "I should treat _____ "
- "I should not _____ "
- "I should try _____ "
- "I should tell _____ "
- "I should _____ "

Surprising or not, we often give away many of our precious hours to other people's projects, goals, and initiatives. We have various reasons for saying "Yes," "Sure," or "I can help," but each time we say "Yes," we say "No" to something else.

Now some have shared with me that these yeses are trade-offs that could appear to align with a future goal, which may be true, but don't forget about the oasis you may be chasing. Be sure you understand what is being asked. How does it align with where you are now or what you are working to align with next?

An easy way to do this is think about the last few times you said "Yes" to an *I should* request that took you more than five hours to complete. How much time did you give yourself to make that decision? Being aware of your yeses can be transformational in your ability to align with more love and light.

To help you determine the best use of your time, check out: Episode 2: "Aligning Your Time and Actions with Your Goals" inside the *Career Strategies for Women that Work* podcast. This popular episode includes a free four-page worksheet that gives direct insight into who, why, and how you are giving away your time. It also offers strategies to help you align with the right work, asks, and requests.

This tool, which I coined "The Power of No" Chart, has given me even more control of my schedule and confidence in my life. The steps are simple, and they bring awareness to your initial responses. I was surprised to learn that most people make decisions in fewer than ten seconds. Whether big or small, we often agree to most asks that come our way, especially at work. I remember years ago that Oprah shared how she takes twenty-four hours to make decisions. I have worked to adopt that strategy for projects, initiatives, and requests for more than five hours of my time. Giving myself the space and time to consider what is being asked of me has helped me align with the right work at the right time.

Here are a few key questions I ask myself before I even consider saying "Yes." They are included in the handout with the podcast mentioned above:

- Is this project in line with my goals?
- Do I know how much time this will take to do it right?
- If I took on this new commitment, would it be for the right reasons?

- How will this new commitment impact my other commitments?
- Are others involved who could impact the timeframes or results of this commitment?
- Do I need more information before I answer?

The worksheet that is included in Episode 2 of the *Career Strategies for Women that Work* podcast also includes four exercises and can be downloaded at https://jjdigeronimo.com/2:

- Exercise 1: What You Have
- Exercise 2: What You Want
- Exercise 3: Focus
- Exercise 4: Checking the Time

Awareness is a great tool you can use to identify where and how you can get some time back into your life so you can explore your inner whispers and seek new ways to unleash your life's work.

Key Finding #13

The "I shoulds" of life deviously take away from our life's work.

CHAPTER 10

SEEKING TO REFUEL

B usy was an understatement, which I wore as a badge of honor. Ridiculous, I know, yet somewhere along the way, I adopted this *external* seeking, which fueled the wrong activities. "I'll get it done," "You can count on me," or "Yes, sure, I can do that" almost became my mantras. I forged ahead with even more to-dos, which brought new deadlines, obstacles, and events that I layered on top of all my other commitments, including those made to my loved ones at home.

After fifteen years of corporate life, with early mornings and many late nights, I was well into my reserve fuel tank. My internal voice was poking me to pay attention. When I had a few minutes of idle time between calls, or after a late-night project was done, I found myself searching the web for retreats—a gathering or experience that promised me an opportunity to reconnect and realign with more meaning. If I had been more self-aware at the time, I would have been more present with the fact that I was searching for opportunities to refuel, realign, and rediscover.

If you are here with me now inside these pages, I assume you, too, are looking for something more fulfilling. Maybe it's a meetup or retreat or experience that provides you with an opportunity to connect with your mind, body, and Soul, or perhaps a break or a time-out from your responsibilities or to-dos.

What are you seeking more of now?

_____

_____

What activities replenish your energy?

_____

_____

What are you being called to add to your schedule?

_____

_____

What do you want to learn more about?

_____

_____

I like this easy question:

The thought of _____ excites me.

If I had more _____, I would _____!

    I was not looking to build or create or even find. I was looking to refuel with space to think and rest, AND with time to remember what made me feel whole, filled up, or even energized. I realized I needed a quiet, beautiful place in nature with peaceful practices that could help me refuel so I would feel alive again.

What does your peaceful place look like?

_____

_____

How does envisioning this place make you feel?

_____

_____

What are you seeking now that can help you feel more energized?

_____

_____

What are you wanting to do, investigate, or seek?

_____

_____

What is holding you back?

_____

_____

For me, guilt and other stories buried deep inside me were keeping me stuck. The daydream of checking out of my life for a few days felt exciting, yet my reality included a color-coded work schedule and two children eagerly waiting for my workday to end. The guilt of leaving them for time off would get the best of me and my daydreams. My family was already adapting to my business travel and frequent late-night conference calls. Asking for more time away seemed unrealistic and selfish.

If I was going to invest in myself for a few days, I first had to acknowledge my guilt and what was holding me back. Once I recognized it, and my definite need to refuel, I could take a better look at my potential options beyond my demanding schedule.

Key Finding #14

Recognizing when you need to refuel is essential.

CHAPTER 11

INTERNAL NUDGES

I did not anticipate an internal tug for something more because there seemed to be a forward momentum in my life and at work. Yet, after years in tech, two startups that had IPOs (initial public offerings), hundreds of plane trips, a husband, and two kids, one would think, "Okay, I'm good." I felt like I did what was expected of me, which should have allowed me the freedom to relax and enjoy the journey, but no, that was not the feeling I was experiencing.

My heart began tugging at me more fiercely. With uncertainty and even annoyance, I often pushed the unsettled feelings away. Instead of listening, I tried convincing myself that I was on the right path, and besides, I was too tired and too far along to change lanes at that point in my life.

After I achieved each notable milestone, my unresolved feelings would again bubble to the surface of my awareness. I would ask myself, *Why do I feel so unsettled?* or *Why is this not good enough?*

Can you relate? Do you have an internal tug encouraging you to look around, seek new information, or explore new avenues in your life? Or do you feel like you have some internal nudges encouraging you to raise your hand, push forward, or take a stand for something bigger than yourself?

What reoccurring conversation do you have with yourself?

_____

_____

What seems incomplete in your life?

_____

_____

What are you yearning for now?

_____

_____

Even when our futures look bright, we still may feel a nudge to seek new information or experiences. While I truly enjoyed my work, the people I worked with, and the leadership opportunities within my tech-related positions and companies, I felt unsettled.

My career goals, set in my early twenties, seemed within reach! Yet the praise and promotions, which used to fuel my tank, did not provide the same momentum and excitement. I beat myself up for months, even years. I often asked myself, *Why can't I be happy or even joyful with what is?* To distract myself from this inner tug, I jumped from book clubs to workout classes to home parties, yet it never seemed to alleviate the reoccurring nudges, nor did it refuel my energy.

When asked, I could not articulate what I was searching for in these groups and gatherings, yet I knew I was craving more meaningful conversations with women. Conversations that activated my desire and their desires to utilize our natural gifts and fuel our goals.

The whispers became thoughts, and I realized I was being guided to create a new community of women. Little did I know then that this would be the launching pad for the work I do now, but back then I felt unsure and scared. I lacked the confidence to create my own gathering, even though I enjoyed creating new things and meeting new people. I was fearful of failing and looking ridiculous among my professional peers.

I tried to get other women to help me or partner with me, and many said they would help, but when the work needed to be done, no one was around to lean on or lean in. Looking back, I now believe this was perfectly orchestrated. I needed to experience every aspect of starting this community from scratch. These were lessons that I leveraged when, a decade later, I took a bigger leap to create a community for professional women seeking Energy Practitioners to refuel, realign, and rediscover. This would not have happened had I not started that earlier community, which is now global.

Yes, I had little time for another initiative, especially one that I had to launch and maintain. However, the reoccurring internal nudges assured me that it was time to act.

As I share in my second book, *Accelerate your Impact*, I pressed forward and, in August 2008, started Tech Savvy Women. It had taken me three years from the time the initial thought appeared because my surges of self-doubt were in my way. Yet finally the day arrived. This gathering created more joy than I ever expected. It was easier than I had envisioned, and the women who attended were grateful and excited. Little did I know, when I was paying the bill for twelve women, that this would be a launching pad that expanded my confidence for many of my future initiatives that would bring women together in meaningful ways.

Key Finding #15

We do not have to know the end state or outcome, but honoring our whispers is a great place to start.

Making time to listen to your nudges and then believing in yourself enough to step forward on those whispers, even if it takes some time, are two instrumental steps that brought me here with you. Many women, including me, want to have everything figured out before starting AND have the confidence that their initiatives will not fail. But this is impossible since it is likely you are starting something new with little experience, especially if you are acting on internal nudges. During my journey, I had to learn how to hear the whispers; how to trust my inner knowing; how to be open to the experience; and how to recognize that my first action might be a step toward something much greater.

What reoccurring thoughts or nudges have appeared for you?

_____

_____

Have you acted on these nudges? Why or why not?

_____

_____

What have you started but stopped because you did not have enough time or confidence?

_____

_____

What is holding you back? Can you describe the fear or reason for self-doubt?

_____

_____

What have you tried to date?

_____

_____

Is there a way for you to start with a few small actions this month?

_____

_____

Is there someone in your life holding you back?

_____

_____

What could you do this month to explore new avenues?

_____

_____

Is there someone you could team up with to ignite your idea or test the waters?

_____

_____

If you, too, are getting ideas, visions, or signs to explore, design, create, or join something, now is just as good a time as ever to carve out a way to explore your nudges. It could be as easy as watching a video, listening to a book, accepting an unexpected invitation, or slowing down to listen to the whispers.

Most of us have a few could-have, would-have, should-have moments...well, maybe drop that *should* and add *desired* moments. If you, too, recognize that you are feeling depleted, sad, or stuck, now is the time to listen, watch, and pay attention to what is coming your way. We often get signs or messages, yet we brush them off because we fear looking silly or not having everything figured out before we start.

I recently met a fabulous woman, who was also a speaker, at a women's event in Kentucky. Connecting with each other's messages, we scheduled a thirty-minute follow-up call after the event to better understand each other's businesses and missions. We spent about two hours on the phone because we had so much to discuss. Dr. Kinga Mnich, social psychologist, educator, and speaker, is widely known for her work helping leaders expand their minds through the power of emotions so they can inspire and lead their teams to success.

Through our discussion, she expressed her passion to create an app that would align women's menstrual cycles with their emotions and actions at work and in life.

Curious, I asked a ton of questions, as I feel that women and their menstrual cycles are a missing piece to the power women hold on our planet. We shared a common passion to remind women about their innate power, so I suggested Kinga lead her talks and research by discussing the power of menstrual cycles.

Kinga's immediate response was, "I'm afraid that my peers won't take me seriously."

I could completely understand her and her response. We have been taught that our periods are bad, dirty, and something that should not be discussed in public.

However, the excitement of taking back our power and showcasing the beauty of our feminine beings is truly exhilarating for me. I believe women are more powerful than we know, and this is one way we have been taught to think less of ourselves. In fact, research was done by the Always/Whisper brand highlighting that educated girls in sixty-five countries lose confidence and self-esteem when they start their periods. To help change the narrative, they started a #LikeAGirl Campaign to rewrite the social rules around girls and puberty. You can find this YouTube video and all other URLs in Appendix A.

I am happy to share that just twenty-four hours after Kinga and I hung up, she sent me this email: "Our conversation was unbelievable. I have everything in my head already mapped out."

What a shift! Two hours of two women discussing their work became a catalyst for addressing our fears about discussing menstrual cycles in professional spheres. This could elevate the frequency of women for generations to come.

I am looking forward to how her work, perspective, and knowing will help us change the way we view our periods, not only for us but for all the girls who are growing up, and for the boys, too!

Many of us know we have gifts, messages, inventions, and all kinds of things buried inside of us. Yes, many of us are on paths that may be fruitful enough, and the thought of changing lanes may seem overwhelming. But what can you explore off the side of your desk, for just a few minutes a day or a few hours a week?

Let me assure you now that you have plenty of time, smarts, and skills. If you are recognizing some gaps in your life, you likely have some ideas about how to fill them. So why wait? What can you do this week, this month, or even today to grow your knowledge, awareness, or excitement about the nudges or whispers you are experiencing?

Key Finding #16

The internal tug may be your guide toward something more meaningful.

CHAPTER 12

FOLLOW THE WHISPERS

The pressure of time seems to be an issue when many of us think about making space for things that excite or inspire us. One trick I use to get out of my own way is scheduling an hour and a half on the weekend, an hour on Tuesday, and thirty minutes on Friday as reoccurring meetings inside my calendar to ensure it happens. It is incredible how much I can research, write, or get done each week during this small amount of time.

To ensure I do not cheat myself of this precious time, I do not allow myself to dismiss these calendar invites and reminders until I spend that allocated time on my whispers and nudges. Three hours a week becomes twelve hours a month, and guess what? That was precisely what I needed to launch a much-needed community!

Yes, I spent less than twelve hours a month creating Tech Savvy Women back in 2008. During those instances, I organized gatherings, took calls, and connected women. Those activities, off the side of my desk, also energized other aspects of my work and life. I later realized that those actions and activities fueled my internal light.

"Fueling My Light" became a term I coined in 2012 for aligning with meaningful activities that make you feel good, whole, and in the flow with things that matter to you. When you fuel your light, you create more momentum and positive energy in other areas of your life.

With a newfound skip in my step, I noticed more collaboration and enjoyment in my daily tasks. I even found myself in more meaningful conversations, and customers began asking about the Tech Savvy Women initiative for the women on their teams.

Part of what motivated me was a desire to crack the code on work-life balance. This drove me to collaborate with other women in my field to find new ways for people to network on a global scale. It also gave me more to talk about on my sales calls.

Today, the thousands of women who belong to this global group share a wealth of knowledge and experience, representing almost every industry and role in technology. The main community resides inside the LinkedIn© group, Tech Savvy Women, which you can check out and join too.

These women are paving the way for more women, young and old, in STEM (Science, Technology, Engineering, and Mathematics) careers. This came as a surprise because this outcome had never been my initial intention. In fact, had I known this, I likely would have allowed my fears to get in my way and I would have never started this community.

At the time I had plenty of fears and also felt lonely, uncertain, and depleted as I tried to balance a young family and a global job. Luckily, I had felt a strong nudge and listened to my internal voice. It was encouraging me to bring women together to share lessons, stories, and best practices. So I started by calling a few women in the industry, simply to meet up for some wine and light snacks. Little did I know it would also fuel my light.

Those who showed up at the first Tech Savvy Women meeting shared their work and their business goals. Throughout the following years, with quarterly meetups, they also shared inspiring words and validated our everyday challenges, which created an undeniable bond.

Our authentic conversations were fantastic and filled with lessons and insights that I thought were essential for younger women. I collected these lessons, and then felt selfish holding onto them. I wanted to write them down so I could eventually share them with my daughter and all the young women I knew who one day would be up against the same issues that we, as women, face today at work and at home—trying to make this *"Having It All"* work.

Unfortunately, finding the time to write the stories down was difficult. My tech career was more than a full-time job, as I led a team that required weekly travel. With young children and a marriage, I felt like time was not on my side.

Yet the voice within would not sit idle for long. It would often nudge me to write. The thought of losing the advice that helped me on my journey was daunting. One night, after finishing a customer proposal, I opened a new document and said to my inner self, "Start with one story." And just like that, my fingers took over.

Exhilarated by what was landing on the page, minutes turned into hours. This exercise of writing one story at a time, a few every week, became a great escape from my other demands, and it was not as huge of a time commitment as I had expected.

So, I have a few questions for you to ask yourself:

As you read this chapter, what is showing up for you right now?

_____

_____

What have you dreamed about that peeked its head out while you were reading?

_____

_____

What could fuel your light with just a few hours a week?

_____

_____

How can you start small, off the side of your desk?

_____

_____

Are there other people who are passionate about the same idea or who can help you on your journey?

_____

_____

If you dedicate a few hours a week now, the thought of _____ excites you!

When I started writing down the stories, I definitely did not think I was writing a book. As I would think about each woman and the lessons I learned, my joy increased. I also loved the vision of sharing what I learned, at some point, with my daughter, who was under five years old at the time.

Weeks turned into months and, like most things, there did not seem to be a straight line of progression. Each step appeared just on time but often not within MY expected timeline. I am laughing as I am sharing this because my expectations of time are certainly a lesson I continue to revisit.

Here are a few key findings I learned from these initial stages:

Key Finding #17

Our life's work is not always as defined as we would like it to be.

Key Finding #18

The next step toward our life's work is often right in front of us.

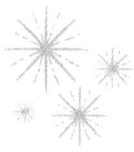

Key Finding #19

It is not always easy, especially for women, as we often want to know why, how, and with whom before we consider diving in and peeling away time from our other commitments.

One of the best lessons is that our life's work is not to figure out the "how." Our life's work is to listen to the whispers we hear and respond to the nudges that are presenting themselves to us.

I was unsure where the nudges and whispers would take me, yet I answered the call to gather the women and write down the stories. My "how" was delivered over a series of months. The Universe eventually provided me with a wonderful editor and publisher.

Months later, twenty-four to be exact, that first story evolved into my first book. Little did I know that my desire to share the stories of women creating their own equations to life would gain so much momentum. After the release of *The Working Woman's GPS: When the Plan to Have It All Has Led You Astray*, the invitations started rolling in to join women's groups and share the wisdom collected and discuss my findings.

Looking back, these off-the-side-of-my-desk activities awakened a dormant desire to get together with women for meaningful conversation. I had no idea that these activities would create a pathway, but they sure illuminated my path for what was ahead.

As you think about your whispers, your interests, or your desires, how can you make some time each week to seek additional knowledge, insight, or connections? Are you up for adding three hours a week—broken down into ninety-minute, one-hour, and thirty-minute time slots, each on separate days—to your calendar as reoccurring meetings with yourself?

Adding these dedicated times to your calendar each week provides not only a commitment to yourself but a sign to the Universe that you are ready to take the next step in your life's work.

Key Finding #20

When we dedicate time to explore our inner whispers, we open the door for more opportunities & synchronicities.

CHAPTER 13

WOMEN WHO HAVE FOLLOWED THEIR WHISPERS

This entire book could be stories of women who made some time to explore their whispers that illuminated their paths. These two women's journeys show a glimpse of the opportunities they have experienced, and I have many more on my podcast *Together We Seek*.

Lynn was well into her health care career with many notable milestones. As she approached fifty, she realized that what used to excite her at work left her desiring more. Her seeking had started three years prior with books and classes off the side of her desk. She eventually took a leap and scheduled one mission trip, and then another. This step took her out of her schedule and created a spark that now refuses to dim, as her desire to work with young women around the world has grown.

When she returned, she spent some time researching local initiatives that aligned with her flourishing interests. She shared her travels and research with friends and co-workers, and in no time, Lynn found a local nonprofit where she could expand her impact.

In addition to her day job, Lynn joined a few nonprofit committees with missions that aligned with her interests. These activities led to new projects and experiences, including working with local officials and emergency medical technicians (EMTs). Her passion for this work was undeniable, and her enthusiasm to make a meaningful difference was contagious. On numerous occasions, the executive director of the nonprofits recognized all her good work as a committee member and then as a leader. Eventually, she was invited to join the nonprofit board. The key word here is *eventually*, as I am often reminded that the Universe does not align with human time.

Excited yet practical, she spent the weekend reviewing her existing commitments. Wanting to be sure she was making the right decision, she spent time in nature seeking internal guidance. Her question: *Should I leap into this new opportunity off the side of my desk, or should I continue to work in the committees that are flexible and less of a commitment?* Uncertain and confused, she continued to ask for a sign. On Sunday evening, she received an unexpected email from her boss that complimented her on recent contributions and mentioned that she should consider additional leadership opportunities. She saw this as the sign she had asked for, and she enthusiastically accepted the board position.

I recently checked in with Lynn. She loves her day-job work and her board position. She shared that she recently sponsored another woman from her committee for a board seat. She also said that she is going back to school on the weekends to obtain an emergency medical technician (EMT) certification, as she felt drawn to that line of work after working on committees with other EMTs.

Lynn's journey reaffirms that the Universe opens up our next steps when we choose to show up in new ways. Her passion for meaningful travel and a desire to help with local initiatives opened many doors for her. She did not want to leave her day job, but like me, she wanted to create more positive energy with meaningful commitments.

This started for Lynn when she felt down, disconnected, and exhausted. If you feel that way as well, why not explore a few things that interest you? If you are not sure how, I suggest paging through some magazines, viewing social media sites, or writing your dreams down. Each year, I work on creating an "energy board" by collecting images that represent how I want to feel inside during the coming twelve months. At the beginning of the year, I hosted an Envisioning Online event where I showed women how I created my energy boards. You can watch the replay for 2022 at www.TogetherWeSeek.Online or grab the full url in Appendix A.

In my experience, the Universe is looking for you to step out of your comfort zone to gain knowledge, set an intention, or express your desires. As you set the wheels in motion for fulfilling your next dream, be aware of what's happening around you. Often, specific items start to fall into place when you verbalize what you are seeking.

One of my favorite stories of the Universe illuminating a path is when a friend of mine and Soul sister, Sharon, an undeclared medical healer, was eager to share her intuitive medical knowing and gifts. She spent decades caring for her three children and their children, along with working and owning a wellness and vitamin store. When nearly sixty, she still felt a burning desire to educate people about herbs and natural supplements that can improve health and treat certain conditions.

At the store, she often answered health questions and knew she had important information to share. With a desire to educate her friends and customers, she wanted to start sending out a weekly email with tips and products that she recommended. With few computer skills at the time, and hours of frustration trying to send a group email, she called me. I helped her as much as I could remotely but eventually mentioned that she could stop by a public library and ask for some free email support.

It took several library visits, but each time Sharon was fortunate to be able to work with her local library's technical lead, Tim. He taught her new ways to use her applications, and eventually, Sharon successfully sent out a group email. Not only was she thrilled with her new confidence, but her weekly emails to friends and customers were well received, generating more conversations and related work.

Tim, who was impressed by her knowledge and content, asked Sharon to be a guest speaker at the library's monthly meeting. Yes, Tim had dual roles. He was the onsite technician and community coordinator.

Sharon accepted and shared natural approaches to good health and hygiene. It was a huge hit, and the library booked her again and again as the crowds grew each month. Years later, she has reached thousands of people with her newsletter. Her monthly talks expanded beyond the library and included numerous local clubs around town and online. Some of her favorite talks include "How to Build a Garden with your Grandkids," "How to Make Natural Toothpaste from Household Products," and "Hosting an Annual Vegan Thanksgiving Dinner." I was thrilled to learn that the state library eventually sent someone to one of Sharon's events so they could replicate some of the activities at other libraries throughout New York State.

What I have seen first-hand and learned through my own work, and the work of other women, is that you never know what will show up when you make time to step into what is calling you. Both Lynn and Sharon had a passion for their side projects and both desired to extend their impact, which drove the mission trips and newsletters.

I share both of these stories with you to reassure you that you do not have to wait to go on a mission trip in another country or spend a lot of money to fuel your light. In fact, Sharon didn't spend a penny to share her knowledge with others, and both women did it off the sides of their desks.

What will you take from these examples?

_____

_____

What knowledge or expertise can you share?

_____

_____

What is an easy thing you can do today to get things into motion?

_____

_____

Is there a hurdle that you can start to work around, somehow?

_____

_____

Magic can happen, but it often does not happen when there is no new action. We can create some magic in our lives at any time, yet we must acknowledge the whispers, make time to explore our interests, and sidestep the doubt that will likely show up. Making time in your schedule to step into what is calling you can be an easy way to fuel your light and align with your life's work.

Key Finding #21

Side projects can fuel your light and illuminate your path.

CHAPTER 14

GROUNDING YOUR PLAN

If you have been working at something for years and have had no helping hands or whispers in your ear or synchronicity in your connections, you are not alone.

I can relate, as numerous times in my life I have had a vision combined with steadfast determination, but no support and no success.

- I started a tech consulting company in 1999 that had no paying customers and closed within six months.
- I spoke at the PMI National Event in 2000, as I desired to be a speaker, and was asked never to apply again because I read from cue cards during my presentation.
- I started an inspirational charm company in 2012 out of my desire to give inspirational gifts. Those gifts now occupy the majority of the space in my work closet.

While I was not afraid to run at my goals hard and fast, many of my initiatives over the decades depleted funds, time, and energy. I felt tired and sad knowing that, at times, I had sacrificed myself and my relationships for endeavors that did not materialize.

Just thinking about those times brings up mixed emotions. My ego feels beat up, yet my Soul knows that these activities were part of my journey and they helped bring me right here, right now, with you, which I would say it's a pretty awesome space to land.

Can you write about a time you worked hard to create a desired result, but it did not manifest?

_____

_____

What lessons did you gain from the experience?

_____

_____

Did you change the entire plan, or did you tweak your direction, goals, or desires?

_____

_____

What part of the experience have you used or benefited from recently?

_____

_____

One lesson I learned a few years ago is to ground my energy before I build a plan or start running at to-dos. This, of course, sounded ridiculous when I first thought of it, but I tried it a few times, and over the years, I have used it at both work and home.

So what exactly do I do? When I have an idea I want to work on, I go outside and state my idea aloud as though the trees, birds, and animals are listening, and then I wait. I wait for some type of sign or acknowledgment from nature. Sometimes the wind picks up, or birds chirp louder, or the glare of the sun shifts.

And sometimes, nothing happens at all.

So many of us get excited about new ideas and start working on them before we take the time to align with an energy bigger than us. An energy that connects all of us and has a flow of white light and love that moves through all of us. This is the momentum I am talking about when I say tap into or align with the flow all around us.

You know this because it is a beautiful feeling. For me, I begin to feel like I am part of a bigger whole. So when I go outside and share my idea, I am looking for an acknowledgment. With this I usually experience a breeze, or hear a recognition from the birds, or witness the sun's light shifting. I see these as validation of an idea and a way to open up my intuition to receive messages, guidance, and input. If nothing happens at all, I think further about the idea and wait for an updated way to approach it before I throw all my effort at it.

During the spring of 2022, I was developing an in-person retreat. The idea had come to me weeks earlier, and on many mornings I would wake up with bits and pieces of how the day could unfold as though I was given these nudges during my sleep. One morning, around 4:00 a.m., I experienced a stream of ideas about the retreat I had envisioned. Even though I did not have all the Energy Practitioners confirmed, I felt compelled to document what the day would look like. With many details racing through my head, I grabbed my phone and started dictating. Within minutes, I found myself writing a description of the day that I eventually used for the retreat's registration page.

Based on previous experiences with these downloads of information in the middle of the night, I knew I may have a difficult time recalling the details later if I fell back to sleep before recording them.

I definitely see these downloads as a sign of support from the Universe. To clarify the Universe's support and this information, I stepped out onto my front porch that following morning. The bustle of the morning was underway; my neighbors were leaving for work and walking their dogs.

I acknowledged those activities around me, and then focused on where my feet where planted. I felt the rays from the sun on my face, as my porch faces east. I took a few deeper breaths, as you do at the end of a yoga class. Then, as if I was asking a friend, I said out loud: "Do you support me hosting a women's event on May 1 with Energy Practitioners to Nurture Our Souls, in Vermilion, Ohio?"

As I finished my ask, I noticed a chirp, which made me smile, and then the trees started to move. Prior to my ask, I did not recognize the wind or even the movement of the leaves, but as I finished my ask, the breeze in the trees gained momentum and generated an undeniable wind that gave me chills. With this additional level of validation, I smiled, waved to a neighbor, and went back inside to work on the retreat.

What do you already do before you start something new? (examples: take a day off, schedule a wellness or beauty service, clean your desk)

_____

_____

How do you prepare for new initiatives? (examples: do your research, write about it, ask questions, schedule meetups, or brush up on best practices)

_____

_____

Which people do you seek out for their feedback?

_____

_____

What new rituals or tasks might you consider implementing before you start something new?

_____

_____

How are you tapping into the unseen support around you?

_____

_____

It is incredible how much support we have available to us for new initiatives and ideas that may not be aligned with our knowing or behaviors. I find many women ask for help—emotional, financial, or mental—from people who do not support their visions or goals. This can leave many of us feeling lonely or defeated before we even start.

So, if you are feeling alone or afraid to ask for assistance, know we have all been there. Today can be the start of your tapping into the energy flow all around you. I encourage you to look beyond what you have known to gain the support and inspiration you need to explore your whispers and follow your nudges. You have all the support you need. It may just come in ways you are not expecting or are not familiar with yet!

Key Finding #22

There is an enormous support system all around us, waiting for us to tap in!

CHAPTER 15

THE GUILT OF ASKING FOR ALONE TIME

A round my fortieth birthday, my career was going well, Tech Savvy Women had been in full swing for more than four years, and my first book was in circulation, generating some buzz. Yet my inner compass was moving to new levels of uncertainty and discomfort.

Admittedly, I had a hard time saying "no," which led to being overscheduled and often exhausted. I pushed through my daily to-do list, keeping busy and productive, but my nagging inner turmoil grew and became impossible to overlook. I was not necessarily looking to get out of my current situation, but I did know that I needed time to explore other fulfilling activities off the side of my desk.

One night, after my husband and children were asleep, I sat in my office, putting the finishing touches on a presentation for a morning meeting. As I was searching for a product description, I found myself revisiting a previous internet query that had led me to a unique solo retreat in Sedona, Arizona. Surprised to find myself on this website again, I clicked around for a few minutes. Within seconds of reading the page, I felt guilt creep in, then flood my body, just as it had the first time I stumbled upon this website. As the guilt rushed through my body, it eventually reached my fingers, and I immediately closed my web browser.

After a few more late-night website visits, I mustered up enough nerve to ask my husband if I could go to Sedona for my birthday. I remember "the ask" as though it was yesterday. With a notable price tag, I felt obligated to ask for his blessing. It reminded me of a time when I was a teenager, asking my parents if I could borrow the car for a party, even though I knew the party was off-limits.

Surprised and uncertain by my ask, I waited as my husband paused for an unusually long time. As I waited for his response, I could feel that familiar guilt exploding throughout my body, flooding every limb. I clenched my fists to distract my mind from answering on his behalf.

Just as I could feel myself ready to add more ancillary details to fill the silence, he said, "I am not sure if we can get childcare for the weekend, but I can ask one of my sisters."

Oh, he's thinking that I'm asking for a couple's weekend to celebrate my birthday. But I need to do this alone. The guilt was overwhelming, yet I knew it was time for some deeper self-discovery.

Time seemed to stand still as I worked through the various ways I could gently share that this was a solo trip. Then he tilted his head, as if expecting me to say more.

This was definitely one of the more unusual conversations in our marriage. I felt obligated to ask because I would be spending a chunk of our family money on a personal exploration trip. With this, my level of guilt soared, and my self-doubt made a master appearance. Even though I made plenty of money in my tech role, I still felt the need to ask, which felt uncomfortable, as I did not fully believe I was worth it. The conversation lingered and leaked into other topics that rotated around commitments and expectations, which I am sure I initiated with my abnormal behavior and need to over-communicate, all stemming from my guilt.

Just as I was ready to retract my ask, he said, "You should go."

I felt my body sink back into my heels out of relief. I was excited, as this was the first step of many in my personal journey to seek answers that could settle my Soul. I have to admit, though, even with his blessing, I second-guessed my decision to go. To manage my guilt about the cost of the trip, I held reoccurring chats within myself about taking him with me.

I later learned that I was not the only person feeling this way about asking for something just for me. Many women yearn to attend events, hire a coach, or go on a retreat yet talk themselves out of it. The list of reasons is endless, but most are anchored in fear and self-doubt that impact their self-worth, so they limit their choices and their actions.

Luckily, it was my fortieth birthday, which felt like a good excuse to prioritize myself. Even so, I considered caving in to my guilt. My mind, ego, and heart had been going at each other for too long, and it was hard to get off that internal hamster wheel. But even while I cringed with guilt, I still booked my travel because I knew I needed help in sorting out what was happening on the inside.

What makes you feel most guilty when asking for or creating some alone time?

_____

_____

What do you feel needs to get done before you are worthy of alone time?

_____

_____

Who do you feel you need to ask to get some alone time?

_____

_____

How do others behave that leaves you feeling guilty about prioritizing your desires? (example: silent treatment, change in attitude, or something else)

_____

_____

What circumstances make it hard to set aside time for yourself?

_____

_____

For many of us, it is not easy to make the time, spend the money, or get help to cover all our demands while taking a much-needed timeout to focus on our life's work. It took me years to make a move and ask for the things I needed to have more alignment and inner peace.

The lesson I learned during this time is: If you do not make the time, no one is likely to do it for you. You are the only one who can make the time to invest in yourself!

Key Finding #23

Giving yourself time to explore your inner knowing is a marvelous gift!

CHAPTER 16

CHOOSING ME

Even with all of my self-created guilt, I was very much looking forward to being alone, away from work and home commitments. I saw it as a time to honor myself as I started a new decade. The day I booked my solo retreat, I felt a surge of energy move through my body like a Hawaiian wave that seemed to wash away my guilt for the moment. It felt so empowering to say "Yes" to me!

These yeses for me were few and far between after I became a mom. I love being a mother, and it is not that I had to ask for permission, yet it seemed that when my first baby arrived, so did the backpack of guilt. Self-induced, I am sure, but I know through my work with women that many of them also grabbed the guilt backpack on the way out of the hospital. I planned to leave this backpack at home during my solo trip to Sedona.

I was not sure what was ahead or how it would unfold, but I knew that booking this retreat was already a huge accomplishment. I had leaped beyond my inner chatter of "I should stay home and go another time." Through this action, I knew I was prioritizing myself, honoring my calling, and leaving a sea of commitments behind, even if it was only for a short time. With this, I felt excited about the possibilities.

When is the last time you felt invigorated by your choices?

_____

_____

What excited you about those choices?

_____

_____

Did you, too, have to leave your guilt backpack, or something else, behind to enjoy these choices?

_____

_____

How did those choices align with who you are?

_____

_____

What did you learn about yourself through those choices?

_____

_____

What in your schedule excites you?

_____

_____

It is not always easy to choose you, especially as you get older and have more responsibilities and people depending on you. Taking time away to refuel and dig into your own thoughts, ideas, and dreams is something only you can give yourself. It is a very worthwhile gift!

Key Finding #24

Sidestepping the guilt is often necessary to prioritize ourselves.

CHAPTER 17

PLANNING FOR A SOLO TRIP

My travel plans were set, and my energy was high. However, I had one last ask—I needed time off from work. I had the vacation time, but my corporate culture was fast-paced and three days off may as well have been three weeks. As I started to draft an email to my boss, I reassured myself that I needed the time and this was no big deal. Deep down, however, I knew this was a big deal. I was shifting. For the first time in ten years, I was making quality time for me, which felt marvelous.

Minutes after my email landed in my boss's inbox, my phone rang. I picked it up and heard my boss blurt, "JJ, where do you need to go for three days?" He hadn't even said a hello.

Without hesitation, I said, "It is my fortieth birthday, and I am going on a solo trip."

He laughed. "Should I take your resignation letter now?"

I almost fell off my chair. *How did he know I was so unsettled? How did he know I was rethinking my current state?* I did not say a peep.

How did he jump into my thoughts?

"Are you there, JJ?" He chuckled.

That familiar flood of guilt rushed through my body like a pack of wild horses that must have taken my tongue. Still, I did not respond.

He hardly let a minute go by when he added, "I mean, you are at mid-life going on a trip by yourself. Sounds like a mid-life crisis. Should I backfill your role while you are gone?"

Realizing I needed to start talking before he made any other plans, I said, "I just need some quiet time in nature so that the next decade is as powerful as this one."

He laughed, and just like that he moved on to some work items.

I now see that my boss's reaction was perfectly orchestrated as another test from the Universe to see if I would take the time to explore my own energy and desires. I have heard many women say that we all play roles in other people's life lessons, and this specific call reminded me of that insight, as he definitely tested my commitment to myself.

A few hours later, I saw my time off was approved. I remember thinking, *Why is it so hard for me to take time for myself? I surely deserve it, but do I believe I deserve it?*

Still uneasy yet excited, I scheduled an evening call with Rick Reynolds, a spiritual guide from Sedona Soul Adventures. This kind and mild-mannered man shared his life and spiritual journey, embracing his gifts of hypnotherapy and emotional freedom technique (EFT), and how he became a spiritual guide. His story and his calm energy put me at ease. We spent most of the time reviewing my Soul Adventure goals, which seemed to focus on my need for clarity. I shared my nagging inner turmoil that seemed to be dragging me to new levels of uncertainty and discomfort within my professional choices. From this, Rick crafted a customized schedule that empowered me to explore vortexes, experience new energy modalities, and meet with fantastic practitioners to help me gain insights and new levels of awareness.

If you are thinking about a solo retreat, take a few minutes to listen to Episode #7: "Solo Trips – Creating Space for You" on the *Career Strategies for Women that Work* podcast at www.JJDiGeronimo.com/7. This episode includes five questions, including what inspires you and what you could do to make it meaningful and purposeful along with other nuggets that could help you on your journey.

Recognizing our feelings, accepting our emotions, and stepping into what is calling us from within is not always easy. But if we can shift our perspectives and view some of our real or perceived challenges as tests, the steps may seem more possible. For me, asking for approval at home and time off from work were tests from the Universe to be sure I was ready for the next chapter in my life's work. Seeing our asks for alone time as commitments to our self-alignment can often enhance our commitments to our work and relationships.

Key Finding #25
We are the only ones who can honor ourselves and our whispers.

CHAPTER 18

EN ROUTE TO SEDONA

As I drove away from the Phoenix airport in my rental car, I felt a bit nervous and scared. Yet I also felt excited as I merged onto I-17 N to Sedona for my first solo trip, seeking new levels of self-awareness. I would like to say that I listened to Carole King or another empowering artist while I felt the wind in my hair, but this was far from my reality. Instead, my day was filled with parking lot conference calls and coffee shop stops to send time-sensitive emails.

This is absurd. My vacation clock has already started.

Yes, my job was demanding. But in reality, I was an overachiever who was afraid to drop any ball, at home or work, that would show any shred of evidence that I could not handle my responsibilities with ease. These self-induced expectations were exhausting and unrealistic and did not provide the self-acceptance I craved. I was operating with the mindset that if I got these tasks done now, I would be able to protect my hours in Sedona, free of disruptions.

I did not realize that my choices to do so much for so many when I should have been carving out time for myself on that first day would eventually become one of my life lessons around being present.

Hours later, as I approached the majestic horizon of red rocks and a stunning sunset, my last email was sent. I remember feeling calm yet enthusiastic about the days ahead. I felt connected to the land and marveled at the incredible natural beauty all around me. I sensed the Universe had been awaiting my arrival.

The following morning, I started my Soul Adventure with a walk around one of Sedona's vortexes, which are visited by people for their spiritual energy. As I sat on a nearby rock, I soaked up the sensations and reviewed my itinerary. Those first few moments felt surreal as I glanced briefly at my schedule and then took in the energy all around me. I felt like I had been waiting a lifetime for this moment.

As the day progressed, I was surprised by how many of the practitioners I met had once held corporate jobs and had been seeking off the sides of their desks. Over a period of years, or even decades, each of them eventually found their way to Sedona. Their gifts were pure, and their passions were evident, with a noticeable recognition of Mother Mary, God, angels, and Jesus in their jewelry, decorations, or the statues around their homes.

I drove all around Sedona as I moved through my self-guided agenda and even over to Cottonwood, Arizona, to explore various practices, visualization exercises, and exchanges that Rick had prearranged. My time in Sedona felt magical. There were lonelier moments as well, when I wished my husband was with me. With awareness of the inner strength it takes to travel alone, I worked to embrace eating solo, driving between sessions, and knocking on the doors of practitioners—who were strangers to me but friends of Sedona Soul Adventures—awaiting my arrival.

As I worked with the various practitioners, I learned how to access energy from the Earth, myself, the stars, the moon, and the sun. I appreciated the quietness of my mornings—something that was hard to come by at home with young kids and demanding deadlines. I found myself walking to breakfast when I could have driven so I could be mesmerized by the skyline and splendor that extended for hundreds of miles. Throughout those two days, I felt supported and loved.

I departed Sedona with a heightened appreciation for every aspect of my journey and for Mother Earth and her vastness. As my plane lifted away from the Arizona ground, I sank into my seat with ease and triumph that I made the time I needed to seek. It was evident that I had been called to Sedona to regroup, realign, and reconnect so I could discover a new level of comfort within myself.

When I deplaned, my internal chatter did not disappear. In fact, at times my ego grew louder, emphasizing the importance of external metrics such as my salary and title and trying to override my emerging purpose. There was no doubt that my mind and heart would put up a good fight for months. During those internal battles, I chose to tap into my memories of my four-hour visit with an angel reader, Stacey Alexander. She reassured me that I had the tools and spiritual support to empower myself and the people I encountered. I put this to the test weekly, asking for guidance and watching for signs and messages.

My life did not change overnight. It took years and many steps, decisions, and compromises to align my physical state with my knowing through activities, meetups, and online sessions that inspired me off the side of my desk.

Each step brought milestones, hurdles, and surprises that required me to embrace the new situation or lesson, even when I did not feel 100 percent ready. Many practitioners and spiritual guides reminded me of:

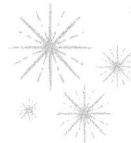

Key Finding #26

Our current situations have a purpose.

Key Finding #27

It is up to us to learn the lessons presented in our lives, as we are right here, right now, for a reason.

While this is not always easy, I have had to learn to ask myself, "Why am I in this place right now?" and "What do I need to learn from this situation?" I have learned that being present provides the attention needed to immerse myself in the lesson, and this helps to move me along on my journey.

This enlightened conversation that circulates around meaning, purpose, and alignment seems more usual in places like Sedona, Arizona, or other spiritual locations such as Machu Picchu, Peru, India, Bali, Indonesia, or within spiritually focused organizations such as the Omega Institute for Holistic Studies and the Kripalu Yoga and Wellness Center in New York State.

I still marvel that my web browser guided me to a place called Sedona Soul Adventures. The website states, "Custom-designed retreat that's all about you, your specific needs, and getting your life on track with Sedona's master healers and practitioners." You may see how my inner knowing jumped at this description. In hindsight, I now know it was the Universe's way of saying, "We've got you."

If your travels usher you this way, be sure to say hello Debra Stangl, the founder, and Rick too. Throughout this book, you may become interested in a practitioner whom I have worked with or met. Please feel free to reach out to any of them. If you have a fantastic guide or energy practitioner who has helped you, please share your experiences at www.TogetherWeSeek.Online so more women receive similar benefits. Many women in my network are looking for recommendations from someone like you.

I suspect that this level of spiritual clarity would have been an enormous step for me had I not grown up visiting Lily Dale, New York. This beautiful community on Lake Erie brings together Lightworkers, spiritual leaders, mediums, and free thinkers. A variety of experiences can be created while inside the private and gated community. If you want to catch a view inside Lily Dale without the cost of a trip, Lisa Ling visited this area as part of her series, *This is Life with Lisa Ling*, which aired on October 28, 2018 and is now available on-demand for a small fee.

This may not seem logical or even normal, but I come from a line of women— my grandmother, mother, and aunts—who each turned to spiritual guidance as a source of untapped information to help make Earthly decisions. This is how I was introduced to Lily Dale. I must admit my spiritual connection was diluted, as I became over-committed in other aspects of my life. Adding the roles of wife, mother, and employee left little time for me and became an array of reasons I used for side-stepping the time I needed to nurture my Universal connection.

At various times in my life, when I felt down or confused or lonely, I was reminded to revisit my practices of journaling, praying, and walking in nature. At times of heightened need, I noticed that new offerings, which could address my yearning for more spiritual assistance, would mysteriously cross my path. I now know those were not accidents.

Key Finding #28

A solo trip can provide the dedicated time for you to explore inside and out.

PART II

REDEFINING
SELF-WORTH

CHAPTER 19

TAPPING IN FROM YOUR DESK

I was back in my suburban life in Ohio filled with work deadlines, school schedules, and other life commitments. Transitioning back into the demands of everyday life after an amazing solo trip was not so easy.

I struggled to stay empowered with an office inside of my home. The demands seemed endless both inside my home office and just feet from my office door, as a list of domestic chores eagerly awaited.

In December 2013, almost a year after arriving home from my Soul Adventure, I was alone, at home, and working on my own as I left my fulltime role, which did not easily align with my ego. Little did I know, my definition of success was driven by my ego, based on fear of not having enough, not being enough, and not being good enough. Being alone without a title or company name or paycheck to lean on left me swimming in my fears.

Looking back, this seems perfectly orchestrated, as my journey to redefine my success metrics likely started years before I landed at this place in time. My Soul was ready for me to partake in more love, gratitude, sufficiency, and completeness aligned to my God-given gifts. My ego was on the defensive and not going to let go without a vicious fight.

The pages ahead include many of the steps I took after I realized the overwhelming level of self-doubt I experienced when I leapt into what I thought was my life's work.

I have been nudged to share these findings with you, even though I do not have it all figured out, as I have discovered new resources, cultivated new conversations, and established new behaviors that have helped me manage my ego. I, we, cannot afford to wait until I feel 100% ready.

Key Finding #29

Now is the time to share, connect, and collaborate, as we all have knowledge that can benefit another.

CHAPTER 20

AN EARLY GLIMPSE OF MY LIFE'S WORK

Little did I know when I was looking across the sea of holiday shoppers that I would get my first clue about my life's work.

The store in the mall was bustling with people grabbing last-minute gifts. The registers were humming, and the checkout line stretched almost out the door. This retailer was known for its jeans and flannel shirts, of which I had a closet full. I worked there throughout high school and returned for long breaks during college.

Even with crazy hours and piles of clothes to refold, I felt privileged to work on the register. My eight-hour shifts slipped away because the checkout line never ended.

One busy Saturday afternoon, when I was still in college, about halfway through my shift, I remember hearing, "You're so stupid," which was followed by, "You're a dumb piece of shit." My radar went up, and I locked eyes with a middle-aged man at least seven people back in the checkout line.

My desire to listen to their exchange distracted me from the customer at my register. I found myself asking my inner self, "*Why was he talking like that to her?*"

As I looked with more intention, I could see that he had a grip on her arm. She was not only looking down, but she was also trying to hide behind a tall stack of sweaters. She was clearly embarrassed as she continued to glance out into the mall.

It was apparent that he noticed me noticing him. I tried to refocus on the customer at my register, but his comments would not stop, and with this added attention, his forcefulness with her intensified. Judging by his public display of anger and her submissive nature, I was sure this was not out of character for him.

As they made their way to my register, I could feel myself wanting to say something. I knew she needed help, but who was I? What could I do?

I questioned myself on how I could help, and before I knew it, I heard myself say, "Does that make you feel good? Do you feel better when you put women down? Do you think it makes you strong? Well, let me tell you, if you have to hurt someone else to feel strong, you are the weak one."

I was just as surprised as they were. I was not expecting to share my inner thoughts about the situation, and definitely not on the Saturday before Christmas when the holiday rush was in full swing.

By the look I saw on his face, I am sure that he did not expect it either.

He turned his energy and focus toward me, and with full throttle, he unloaded.

I could feel his words spray my face and his energy engulf my body. I cannot even recall what he said outside of, "Mind your own business, you stupid girl!" along with lots of vulgar swear words.

The exchange was over in a few brief minutes. My body buzzed with unexpected unsettled energy as my manager Margie swiftly guided me off the register and to the back of the store.

In the breakroom, I felt embarrassed and nervous. I questioned my actions and was fearful he would come back.

A short while later, as I returned to the floor, I was notified by a co-worker that I was demoted to the fitting rooms for the rest of the week. That was the least desirable role in the store, but, at that point, I did not care.

I started beating myself up on the inside. I realized that I could have worsened that woman's situation that day, and it sickens me to think about what happened to her after they left the store. I am sure he took out all his frustration on someone, probably her, which still saddens me.

What I know for sure is that seeing her verbally abused by that dark energy enraged me. Her lack of a voice was evident, and I knew her situation was dire because I had noticed marks on her arms when they were at the register.

I still wish I could have done more for her at the time, but I was naive. I lacked the awareness of the dynamics of abusers. I now know that going head-on with one of these people is not the recommended approach. Instead, trying to help the victim should be the priority. I have since learned that the abuser will often try to distract a person from trying to talk with the victim.

Although I was young and inexperienced during this exchange, I was hopeful that standing up to him gave her a glimpse of possibilities.

As I share this story with you, my heart still sinks with sadness as I think about what might have happened to her and the many women in terrible situations that suppress their confidence and muzzle their voices with a vortex of fear.

I could definitely bring myself to a dark place in minutes if I allowed myself to follow that energy, but now I choose to focus on what I can impact, what I can do, and who I can help. I donate to local and global programs that help women and children move out of abusive situations. I also have held meetings with women in Uganda through Willow International. The first sentence on their About page on their website states: "There is light that drowns out the darkness." Willow International's mission is "to eradicate human trafficking. Through survivor care, government reform, and global partnerships, we can erase this plague and restore hope to the millions of victims across the globe."

Beyond this, I mark that situation, that day, as a beacon of light in my life journey and work. With more than forty people in the store that day, at that specific time, witnessing the same exchange, why was I, a twenty-year-old woman, one of the only people to have an outward reaction?

Why did his actions toward that woman ignite me?

Why did I feel so compelled to speak up?

Why did I shake with fear for hours afterward?

Yes, many have shared that little to no good could come from speaking up, but I am not sure I had a choice. My inner self was activated, and doing nothing was not an option. Looking back on that day, it marked the beginning of my journey toward unleashing my inner light. This situation marked a new desire to support women in a public setting.

Key Finding #30

We get sneak peeks into what ignites our Souls.

CHAPTER 21

SEEDS OF INSIGHT

Many of us captured glimpses of our life's work, often starting at an early age. These glimpses of your life's work could be a memory of something that makes you happy, upset, curious, angry, or satisfied. These experiences and related feelings can shed light upon some level of insight, knowing, or energy that illuminates your passions.

These are usually rather memorable moments or experiences, as they often create more than a passing emotion—just as I have been able to recall the series of events back from my retail days that occurred almost thirty years ago. These experiences often invoke a full-body memory.

Let's take a few minutes to think about a time in your life when you recall a full-body reaction:

_____

_____

Maybe you've had a few:

_____

_____

Take a minute to reflect on these moments. And, if you cannot think of any, think about a time you were filled with joy.

Can you make any correlation between how you felt in those moments or situations and what is important to you now?

_____

_____

Experiences, events, or situations that you remember, with a full-body reaction, could be beautiful, like Susan's experience at Bristol Hills in Bloomfield, New York.

Flowers have always brought Susan so much joy. Her mom had always called her the "flower girl," and she even remembers her first flower, an iris.

Fast forward decades. Flowers became Susan's escape from her reality after the passing of her husband.

To manage her grief, she created a memorial garden that began with a topiary-shaped lilac tree. She then added hydrangeas and tree peonies bulbs. When she could find time away from her work and her family, she found herself planting and expanding her flower garden.

As her story unfolds on her website, Susan shares that when she gardened, the layer of ice around her heart melted, preparing her for the next chapter in her life. She met a new love that eventually became her husband. He encouraged and supported her in planting her dream, a lavender farm.

I stumbled across Susan's lavender farm on a beautiful October Monday en route to celebrating my mom's seventy-fifth birthday at The Lake House Hotel on the Finger Lakes in the middle of New York.

We were driving along at fifty-five miles per hour when my mom and I noticed her lavender sign nestled in the front of a large yard with an oversized barn. It was not easy to hang a U-turn, but we were determined. I turned the car around on the next street, and we made our way back to Susan's long driveway.

We saw her bent over with her head in one of her many gardens. She looked surprised to see us pulling in but hand motioned us up to the top of the driveway adjacent to her three-story white barn. When we opened our car doors, she was already introducing us to her nephew and then to her dog, whose dirty paws and wet head gave the impression that he had spent the morning on his own adventure.

We had not realized the farm was closed to visitors, yet Susan welcomed us in. She graciously answered all our questions about her farm, her business, and her life's journey. As we walked the farm, she shared her stories and educated us on the different lavender plants. Seeing the results of all of her hard work, we were eager to take a piece of her farm with us.

Susan walked us into the big white barn, where she hosts events and even designs programs where people can make wreaths and other flower-based products.

My mom and I were in our glory as we shared in her energy and journey. We collected a bag full of the best-smelling lavender candles I have ever burned.

As we were getting back into our car to leave, Susan shared that she had been unsure she could create a lavender farm, but she credited her now-husband, who had graciously said, "Susan, you could go get another degree, but what would you love, love, love to do?"

Susan responded with, "I always wanted a lavender farm."

He said, "Then I will help you build that lavender farm."

In just a few years and with lots of hours on the farm, Susan has more than 2,000 lavender plants. She shares her love for flowers with people worldwide and creates flower arrangements and bouquets for birthdays, bridal showers, baby showers, and weddings.

What events or situations in your life give rise to an undeniable level of emotion, either good or bad?

_____

_____

What events or situations in your life would you like to revisit or expand?

_____

_____

What have you talked yourself out of that you may want to revisit?

_____

_____

I, of course, had no idea while working retail that three decades later, I would see my holiday encounter with an abuser as a milestone in my life's work. Or I would be referencing it as a beacon of light for the work I now do to empower women to step into their light, gifts, and knowing.

And even though I do not see women being emotionally or physically abused right in front of me that often, many women who cross my path carry stories, situations, or histories that hold them back or even down, keeping them from stepping into their potential and their life's work.

What may be holding you back?

_____

_____

If someone you love says, "I will support you. What do you want to do?", where would you align your energy and your time?

_____

_____

What excites you about what you thought about or wrote above?

_____

_____

Make time to think about events or situations in your life that may have given you insights about your passions, interests or frustrations. These are often accompanied by a spike of emotions.

It is no mistake this book landed in your hands. Your focus is shifting. You are ready for your next chapter, but you likely have to realign some of your energy and reassess some of your stories to make space for that shift.

I am honored you are here and thrilled to be sharing some of these tools with you to help you make more room for love, light, and new levels of impact!

Key Finding #31

There are seeds of insight tucked away, waiting for your attention.

CHAPTER 22

DOUBTING OUR CHOICES

E ven with glimpses of our work at an early age, many of us do not immediately leap into our natural talents. As we move through grade school to high school, we are inundated with messages, expectations, and experiences that encourage us to find our calling but that often come wrapped in the expectations society places on women. This is a topic I discuss in great detail in my book *The Working Woman's GPS, When the Plan to Have It All Has Led You Astray.*

Women receive both conscious and subconscious messages about their worth and what it means to be a woman all day, every day. In an effort to be successful—whatever that means—you might have leaned into a path that may or may not align with your talents and gifts.

Over time, you may experience some discomfort with your choices or question your alignment at work and in life. You may change jobs, zip codes, friend groups, or relationships, which may create some contentment for some time.

Eventually, however, when you begin to shift your focus from collecting titles, salaries, and accolades on the outside to digging through your stories on the inside, the real work starts. These stories often act as anchors that lock us into thoughts and patterns that influence our actions and choices.

Recognizing and releasing internal stories that keep you in a holding pattern often does not happen on its own. There is usually a catalyst that kickstarts the process. You might live through a breakup, job change, kids arriving or leaving, or a loved one passing away, and suddenly, knock-knock, an overwhelming desire to do things differently shows up at your door!

One of my more instrumental awakenings arrived when I gathered enough courage and leaped from my corporate role to embark on my own full-time business. I was scared and second-guessed myself every day before and after giving my notice. I talked with friends, journaled, and drove my husband and business coach nuts, as I had to talk through every possible scenario, few of which came true.

It seemed like the right time—company layoffs and reorgs made it easy to close an eight-year chapter and move toward my work with women in business. While I was nervous about moving out on my own, I was excited to see what I could do. I told myself often that I could always go back into technology. This gave me the reassurance I needed to step into the unknown.

I was passionate about sharing my research and findings to help working women make their goals a reality. Yet I was also unsure of myself because a few of my co-workers mentioned that I could only leave because my husband had a good job. While this was true, I had been saving funds, and my reason for taking this leap had nothing to do with my husband's salary. I was prepared to jump back in if this work could not stand on its own. Even with this doubt from others, I knew I had to make the shift.

I worked long hours as I moved from specialized work in cloud computing to wearing every hat in my own business as an author and speaker working toward being a voice for women in business. I had a lot to learn about the industry and stabilizing my business. I did not initially realize that I was about to embark on a huge life lesson, as the knocking was subtle.

As I worked inside my accounting software each month, I could hear a lingering voice. *This is not working. Bad choice to leave your day job.* I was questioning my decisions constantly. My discomfort and self-doubt appeared in every purchase, booking, and transaction.

It did not take me long to realize my internal story: "I will be worthy when I have, make, or earn more money." I obviously still had some self-worth hurdles to deal with when it came to finances.

Being aware and open to new levels of knowledge is always a possibility for us, but it often takes life events to create the space within us for the Universe to squeeze in some new insights. I had many reoccurring moments of negative self-talk that all came to a head about eighteen months out on my own when I lost a big opportunity that I had been working on for more than twelve months. I seemed unable to crack the code on my revenue streams. I felt really down on myself and my choice to step out on my own. I felt like I had made the wrong decision leaving my corporate work. I was tired, depleted, and so hard on myself that it just did not seem worth it.

This disappointing news overshadowed an upcoming family road trip. I found myself trying to push away the critical voice inside of my head that was beating me up pretty consistently. In my frustration about the state of my business and instead of packing, I decided to pick a project with quick and easy results: unloading the dishwasher.

I turned on one of my favorite shows, the Emmy award-winning *Super Soul Sunday*. To my surprise, the topic of money was being discussed. I found myself walking over to the TV remote, rewinding, and listening again. The words I heard were both powerful and aligned with exactly how I was feeling. I was struck by deep wisdom that seemed to rattle my inner critic.

The show's guest's voice was soft yet firm, and her words "not enough" echoed in my head, seeming to cinch the source of my feelings of inadequacy. I had been struggling as an entrepreneur, even while doing the work I love. However, leaving my high-paying corporate job to "try it out," or—in my other words—"make a bigger impact," seemed to be leading me down a familiar path to failure.

Every day after I left my paycheck, I had questioned my value. I was not making enough money, or at least not the money I had expected.

And just when I thought I was near the end, a well-known activist and author crossed my path while unloading the dishes with the exact wisdom and insight I needed to pull myself out of my self-loathing, money-focused talk track. It was Lynne Twist, a bestselling author, discussing her award-winning book, *The Soul of Money: Transforming Your Relationship with Money and Life.* At that moment, she was a gift to me from the Universe that reset my perspective and challenged how I told myself my stories before making decisions.

Her words felt so liberating because they addressed the popular mantra, "There is not enough money." This was the primary story that played on repeat inside my head and had influenced a large portion of my actions. Her insights became a true catalyst for change within me.

Key Finding #32

Money often influences our thoughts, actions, and choices.

CHAPTER 23

MONEY IS THE HURDLE FOR MANY

Through my work with women, I have learned that I am not alone in my self-doubts around money. Many women are eager to step out in new ways, create new chapters in their books of life, or start something off the sides of their desks yet are staying in their roles, relationships, and situations because of the hold money has on them. Can you relate?

What decisions do you make based on money?

_____

_____

How does money keep you in a stand-still situation?

_____

_____

The lack of money, the fear of not having enough money, and the belief that there is not enough—these money stories were programmed into me at an early age. Now I work to intercept these beliefs before they trigger my actions.

What money-related stories do you have playing on repeat inside your head?

_____

_____

When or how have you been conditioned to chase, hoard, or overspend money?

_____

_____

A belief in the scarcity of money has many of us in a holding pattern. The fear of letting go to make room to spread our wings is real. Many, many women sit and wait to make their moves, and sadly, a fear-based mindset rarely produces that opportunity. So they wait, and years disappear.

These human-made fears are the reality for so many of us. I may even go so far as to say money, for many, blurs our light and potentially our life's work.

Sure, money can keep us off the streets, but does it require us to tie our self-worth to it? Or, is money an illusion? Or an exchange mechanism to which we give away too much of our power?

How much power do you give money in your life?

_____

_____

As I was growing up, I heard endless family conversations and fights about money, and saw disappointments and celebrations revolving around it. We were not the poorest in our zip code, but we had our fair share of church cheese and lottery dreams. Naturally, at an early age, I adopted a belief that there was never enough money.

To ensure I avoided a lack of funds, I created a daily creed to collect money. Little did I realize that even with an abundance of funds, I was still allowing the energy of money to manipulate me as it did my family. The feelings related to money continued to shape my decisions and happiness as I moved through my life.

I am now certain that this established childhood experience set me up for my success mantra, which I previously referred to as an oasis of power, wealth, and recognition. My fear of not being enough likely fueled this equation. This makes me slightly nauseous now, as I realize it was ALL outward focused.

The not-so-funny thing, since I grew up without money, was that I had no idea how to manage or leverage the money that I eventually earned. In fact, in 1998, I became a millionaire, as I was part of a high-flying tech company that made its initial public offerings (IPO). Sadly, I lost every penny because I never sold the thousands of shares in stock granted to me when I started with the company as employee number 48. My strike price for the thousands of shares I owned was $37, and the price rose to more than $800 a share. In hindsight, I now realize I was afraid of not having money AND had no idea what to do with the money that came my way.

Key Finding #33

It is important to learn how to cultivate healthy activities and thoughts around and with money.

I had no knowledge or process for growing, protecting, or using the money I collected for good purposes. My main driver around money was to collect it, in fear of not having it, to relieve the discomfort or joylessness of not having enough.

Looking back, I needed a little more Suze Orman (an American financial advisor, author, and podcast host) in my life. She said, "The only way you will ever permanently take control of your financial life is to dig deep and fix the root problem." It was evident from my actions that I had made no time to learn how to effectively manage or leverage the money I was making. I was too busy avoiding poverty and the related feeling of not having or being enough.

How do you view money in your life?

_____

_____

Do you see money as a tool to nurture what is important to you?

_____

_____

I did not realize when I downloaded Lynne's book *The Soul of Money*, just before our family trip, that I was about to embark on an exploration of one of my self-worth stories. My money stories were confusing my self-worth, as they were buried deep in my subconscious mind, and my ego would serve them up anytime I was ready to step out in a new way.

To tame these stories, I carved out an hour each day during our family trip to listen to Lynne's words as I walked the maze of paths near our rented house. Her insights helped me understand how I thought about money. Here are a few of my key learnings from her work that may resonate with you, too.

- "As a society, we give money so much power—we have assigned it more power than human life."
- "We swim in a culture of 'there is not enough.' Not enough sleep, friends, vacations, or time. This creates a toxic state for us that drives 'I am not enough.'"
- "This 'not-enough' society has us chasing what we do not have and not appreciating what we do have. This drives us all to a place of being dissatisfied and feeling like we are not enough."

For me, this book was eye-opening and even mind-blowing. Her knowledge was so comforting, and it was wrapped in such wisdom. I never considered using money as a tool to advance causes that were meaningful to me. Lynne inspired me to view money as a way to illuminate my future momentum.

I have recommended this book to hundreds of people because her teachings about what money is and is not hit me in my core. It changed the way I think about money, especially how I collect it and what power I give to it. Her words and frequency seeped into the depths of my Soul. They empowered me to transform my outdated behaviors around money that had acted as shackles, keeping me from what was possible.

This level of awakening highlighted my deep fears around my funds. I realized I had to change my self-talk and reset my perception and alignment with money. The most profound lesson she shared was her explanation about the flow of money and how important it is that we move money around to advance the things that are important to us. I had never before considered using money as a tool to assist causes that were meaningful to me.

I had not been expecting such an awakening. In fact, I am certain that I had heard of Lynne years before on Oprah's ABC show, but it was not the right time for this lesson because it did not grab my interest or resonate with my Soul. However, this time I was ready for it. I had been working for a few years to unlock my inner knowing, step by step and resource by resource. When this crossed my path again, I became intrigued. My Soul heard the calling, and this time, I made the time to listen, learn, and adjust. Committing to taking walks with an audiobook gave me the mental freedom to seek knowledge, create a new level of awareness about my past relationship with money, and open myself up to a healthier future.

Key Finding #34

Money harnesses the power you give it.

CHAPTER 24

MONEY – ABUNDANCE
OR FEAR

Many people struggle to find their self-worth without incorporating money, a title, or an association in some way to validate or acknowledge themselves. These external metrics, often coupled with other people's expectations, form the basis for how we talk to ourselves. These internal stories, created through our experiences—some even developed decades earlier—can linger and resurface as new situations present themselves.

These talk tracks and self-defined mantras related to not having enough or being enough can act as constraints. For many of us, they can even restrict or bind us to jobs, situations, and relationships that prevent some of us from fully stepping into our truest selves and potentials.

Lynne Twist's lessons about scarcity, sufficiency, poverty, and abundance opened my heart and mind to how I perceived money and how I allowed it to set the metrics of success in my life. Lynne's books, in addition to many of her articles, including "The Surprising Truth of Sufficiency," posted on December 17, 2009, are just some of the many resources that altered my thoughts and my actions, and eventually shifted my success metrics.

Here are some questions I wish had been part of life-preparation classes in high school or college, OR that my financial planners had taken the time to ask:

How do you view money? (Do you associate it with abundance or fear?)

_____

_____

When does money hold the most control over you?

_____

_____

How do you like to spend money?

_____

_____

In what ways do you spend money to feel good?

_____

_____

How do you use money as a tool to create meaning in your life?

_____

_____

How is money aiding or hindering your goals?

_____

_____

When does money hold you back?

_____

_____

Would you consider reading _The Soul of Money_ by Lynne Twist?

_____

_____

For much of my life, I gave money the wrong power. I had often let it control my decisions and define my self-worth. My view of money was unhealthy and unproductive and it fed my childhood-provoked fear of not having enough. Money affected many of my choices and beliefs. I had not considered viewing income as a tool or using it to advance initiatives or activities that were important to me.

How do you feel about money?

_____

_____

Who taught you about money?

_____

_____

Does money hinder your desired actions and alignment?

_____

_____

Do you need to revisit your money stories?

_____

_____

It took some time for me to envision money as a wave of energy or a frequency; as a positive light to share; or as a tool I could use to support a mission, company, brand, group of people, or an eco-friendly initiative.

Envision money as an activator that infuses energy into things that are important to you. You can see it as the heat needed to fly a hot-air balloon.

What does life look like for you if you can infuse heat into your aspirations, goals, or whispers?

_____

_____

What obstacles would you like to rise above and fly over?

_____

_____

This mental shift of viewing money as a tool has helped me shift my perspective on how to use it. As a frequency that you work within, it can be used as a band of energy that feels good and a resource you share to empower whatever is important to you. This shift in the way I now view money is beautiful, meaningful, and impactful.

Embracing the idea that money is a frequency and an exchange of energy, support, and inspiration is so much more rewarding and purposeful. I much prefer this way of being over "I need more," "It defines me," or "I am in agony because I have to hoard it out of fear."

Key Finding #35

Money, and the energy you align with it, can infuse or defuse your whispers.

CHAPTER 25

MONEY CARRIES THE FREQUENCY WE GIVE IT

Your relationship with money is only altered when YOU decided to dig into your stories and the feelings you assign it. It's time to check in with yourself: Are you giving away your potential impact to an artificial energy that our society has given to pieces of paper?

When you do not decide for yourself, sometimes your choices decide for you. In my case, leaving a dependable paycheck created a huge awakening on so many levels that illuminated my money issues. Even though I saved for six years and my husband's business continued to grow, I struggled with my relationship with money. Many friends and business strategists suggested I write down my money goals and my financial milestones and track them weekly. However, this advice stifled my work because it put me right back into the familiar rat race of chasing the oasis of success, which included money, power, and access.

Even if your spouse or family can support you, it does not mean all your money stories and hang-ups fall away. In fact, this financial safety net may cause you to further hide or distort your relationship with money.

In my marriage, I struggled, at times, with the term "our money." Along the way, I created stories in my head that I had to directly earn the money I spent. The opposite can be true as well—some carelessly spend others' money, and some even base their self-worth on the money others spend on them. Regardless of where you are with money, most of us have some story related to money that impacts how we spend, use, and view it. In fact, I have heard many, including talk show host Oprah Winfrey, share that money puts a magnifying glass on your insecurities and even shortcomings.

How can you start to see that there is more than enough money to go around? Lynne Twist's *The Soul of Money* started my deep investigation into my relationship with money—both my spending habits and how I felt about it.

Then, three years after I put Lynne's practices into action, a book by Denise Duffield-Thomas crossed my path, further expanding my awareness about the role money played in my life. That book is called *Get Rich, Lucky Bitch! Release Your Money Blocks and Live a First-Class Life.*

Denise suggested starting with little steps that can be taken every day. Her advice was to give gratitude for every little thing that came my way. She reminded me that the Universe will bring us exactly what we need, in abundance, if we appreciate what we have right now.

 ### *Key Finding #36*

I am rich in resources, knowledge, friendships, and love.

Practicing gratitude can be hard to do because marketers flood our surroundings daily with reminders about what we do not have, what we "need," or what will supposedly make us feel better about ourselves. If we are always yearning for more or disappointed with what we have now, the Universe is not going to give us more. So, we must do our part by recognizing all that is already coming our way and contributing in a meaningful way.

Working to shift our focus onto the abundance that already exists is key to cultivating more desirable energies. Appreciation of what we already have creates opportunities for higher frequencies and more abundance.

Yes, it may be hard to believe that there is more than enough abundance, especially if things are not going your way, but YOU MUST count your blessings.

What has the Universe provided you with today, and even yesterday, that you could consider abundance? This could be a card, a meal, an unexpected message, a call, a gift, insights, or even a penny lying in the parking lot. It takes practice to recognize all that is available for us right here and now.

Key Finding #37

There is abundance all around us.

I found I had to develop a mental awareness to acutely notice the messages, signs, gifts, and experiences all around me. To get started with retraining my mind, I created prompts to use during the first ten days. This began with writing down a daily list of gifts that came my way. Just like me, your first reaction may be, "I do not have time for this." Remember, however, that this practice piggybacks on almost all these lessons because it is a great step toward being present and feeling grateful for what you already have. And if you are thinking, "I do not have any abundance in my life," the first thing you may need to shift is your perspective and awareness of what is happening right now all around you.

If you are ahead of that step, you know that "being present" is key to many of the lessons related to fulfillment that fuel your light and life's work. This means you are careful and aware of how you're spending your time. You are not allowing your mind and ego to rob you of the current moment. And, you are present, in the moment, looking, watching, and paying attention to all the things happening in your path, as this is where you will experience, see, and appreciate the many gifts that come your way.

I'll bet you have more beautiful things happening each day than you realize. Noticing and listing out all the abundance and love that comes your way can create momentum for more love and abundance.

I copied the following ten reminders into my calendar at 7:00 a.m. each day for ten days to be sure I was on the lookout as I started my day. I expected to collect ten ways I received abundance each day, and these prompts helped me stay focused.

I do not dismiss a task until I have completed it, even if it takes me all day to get it done. This shift in my focus has been helpful in all aspects of my life because I have conditioned myself to constantly look for abundance. (Listed in Appendix: C)

Day 1: This is how the Universe has sent me love and abundance today

_____

_____

Day 2: Look at the abundance the Universe has shared with me today

_____

_____

Day 3: Big and small, I can see how I am showered with love from the Universe

_____

_____

Day 4: I am seeing the synergies in my day and the love from the Universe

_____

_____

Day 5: I am surprised by how many little things the Universe sends my way each day

_____

_____

Day 6: I am seeing the focus shift right before me, as abundance is everywhere

_____

_____

Day 7: I am grateful that I have taken the time to log all that the Universe sends my way

_____

_____

Day 8: Lucky me—I am now more aware of my blessings

_____

_____

Day 9: What I focus on expands; the abundance is showing up in so many ways

_____

_____

Day 10: I am unique, beautiful, and full of the abundance I need to do my work

_____

_____

Doing this for ten days and beyond is often necessary to shift the view and mindset associated with the abundance in your life. In fact, I keep a folder inside my inbox called "AHHHHHHH" and have a wall in my office where I hang up tokens of all the love that comes my way. I save all the moments that I am receiving from the Universe from various people, events, and experiences.

I am blessed. You are blessed, too, with abundance, love, and access to a frequency that will illuminate your path based on your gifts and desires. As you collect your abundances each day, you can say your own prayer of gratitude or use mine:

"Thank you for the abundance in love, connections, experiences, and growth. I feel rich from the energy I create, share, and receive within my work and throughout life."

Key Finding #38

It is a choice to experience the abundance and riches all around you.

CHAPTER 26

SHIFTING INTO ABUNDANCE

I struggled with my perception of, connection with, and self-talk about money for years. The structure of the internal dance circulated around having enough money but leaked into related efforts, taking the joy and fun out of many moments.

Fortunately, my lifelong friend and spiritual guru, Beckett Johnson, weighs in with great insight whenever I ask. Our friendship started back in the eighties with our love for soccer and song lyrics. Fast forward over four decades, and now we share book titles, inspiring videos, spiritual findings, and great learnings.

When sharing the key findings from the last few chapters as they were unfolding in my life, Beckett shared, "JJ, focus on the energy and frequency you create, maintain, and exchange with others and not on the money you collect."

His comment came at just the right time like an angel whispering in my ear. It may sound simple or even silly, but my lessons and his words collided at just the right moment, creating a mind shift.

I loved it so much that I created a one-page reminder in 72-point font with this key finding and taped it to the wall in my office.

Key Finding #39

Focus on the Energy You Exchange.

With this new level of awareness and permission, I felt empowered and even liberated. I am not sure if it was timing or the pinnacle of all my money work, but his words arrived just in time within a guided moment that still has a direct effect on my levels of joy and impact.

With this new direction and my openness to a shift in the way I viewed money, I focused my mindset on the abundance of energy and frequency I received. With this change, I received more invitations, testimonials, and even better reviews.

It seemed that my upgraded frequency was taking center stage with new exchanges and conversations with others. I found myself coming from a place of greater authenticity and more abundance, which allowed me the space and energy to increase my confidence in aligning with my life's work.

This also heightened my focus on activities and actions that I think had an indirect influence to elevate the divine feminine energy of the planet, from new women that crossed my paths, to invites I received and conversations I found myself within. I had clear indicators that the way I engaged with the world around me was shifting.

I now realized as I am sharing these findings and experiences with you that all these lessons and related work were necessary and needed to start with me first. With this advice from my dear friend coinciding with Lynne's book and Denise's emphasis on abundance, I spent the next few years altering my focus, stories, and beliefs around money.

What money stories do you visit that hinder you and your journey?

_____

_____

What stories around money are no longer serving you?

_____

_____

What money stories do you need to work through to let go?

_____

_____

In what ways can you view money differently to empower your whispers?

_____

_____

For many of us, money is a focal point that impacts how we feel about our lives, work, and contributions, which is why I've spent several chapters on the subject.

Since early on in my life, I have been tested many times when it comes to how I view and use money. It has taken dedicated effort and time to shift my scarcity mindset into empowering energy that uses money as a tool to create momentum and impact.

The shift has been its own journey that has allowed me to recognize the abundance of joy, self-love, and celebrations all around me. I now recognize that money is a tool to advance things that are important to me.

Giving yourself tools to investigate what you value and better use what you already have can illuminate your gifts to help you uncover your life's work. Sometimes your insights will arrive through the people who cross your path or have been in your life. Be open to their gifts, whether it is a book, a resource, or a direction that will guide you toward your next step.

Key Finding #40

Learned beliefs take time and curiosity to shift.

CHAPTER 27

GRATITUDE FOR YOUR GUIDES

When I was in high school, I was lucky to have a dedicated guidance counselor, Mr. Mancuso. Although my ACT and SAT scores were low, due to an undiagnosed case of dyslexia, he actively encouraged me to go to college.

Looking back, his investment was one of those guided moments in life in which I could have gone left, but his momentum and sponsorship pushed me right. I may have eventually aligned my life in that direction, but I suspect it would have taken me years to get on this path without his genuine help and belief in what was possible. To this day, I am grateful for the guidance he provided for my journey, at a time when I needed a supported vision for what was possible.

Can you think about a few people in your life who guided you toward a meaningful direction?

_____

_____

How were some of these guided moments instrumental in your journey?

_____

_____

What energetic gratitude can you share with them, from where you are right now, regardless of their location?

_____

_____

It may only be one person, or it may be many; the number is irrelevant and so is the depth of your relationship. The support and love you experienced and the gratitude you have for your guides is the experience you want to capture right now.

Key Finding #41

Guides come and go; sometimes the interaction is for a few minutes, and other times, the relationship is for a lifetime.

A few months ago, I drove back to my hometown and hosted a dinner for six people who had guided me through my instrumental teenage years. I wrote each person a personal note describing how they guided me to the place I am today. At dinner we shared stories and I gave them some meaningful gifts. There were hours of laughter and some tears—it was a touching evening. However, my gratitude stretches far beyond this event and will be carried in my heart for years.

If you feel inclined, take a minute to write a note, create a social media post, or think about something you can share in honor of one or more of your guides. The feelings or energy for these guides is usually filled with appreciation, as these guides have often gone beyond what is expected to provide information, support, suggestions or even nudge you in a specific direction.

If you are inspired, think of someone for whom you can act as a guide right now. Yes, it could be family, but how about a neighbor, babysitter, waitress, or someone who would not expect it? This can be a way for you to pay it forward, especially if you cannot get in touch with those who have been your guides in the past.

An amazing example of how to be a positive, life-changing guide for many is Jimmy Malone, a local radio personality in Cleveland, Ohio. We crossed paths more than ten years ago when my husband and I were looking for nonprofits that supported kids in need.

He met us at a local diner. After we ordered, he opened a Target photo envelope. Much to our surprise, he had about seventy-five pictures, one for each student who was in his college scholarship program. He shared some about their backgrounds, colleges, GPAs, degrees, years of graduation, and scholarships each one had received. His passion and dedication were indescribable. We were more than eager to contribute to his mission. He created Malone Scholarship with April Malone in 1993, and their daughter, Angela Malone, soon joined the mission too.

Each year, Jimmy hand-selects about twenty high school students with stellar grades but who also have life situations that stifle their college dreams. Many have unstable family units with parents who are incarcerated or dependent on illegal substances. Some of these students have parents who passed away or parents who have left and never come back, leaving them to the foster care system, with relatives, or to fend for themselves. With the Malone Scholarships, these students thrive despite their challenging childhoods, unstable situations, and unpredictable housing arrangements.

Many of their stories are heartbreaking, yet the perseverance of these students is inspirational. Jimmy is, for many, my Mr. Mancuso—a guide who helps them pick schools and align funds and who acts as a mentor for the duration of their college years.

When Jimmy shared stories about his students, it was quickly apparent that this off-the-side-of-his-desk project fuels his Soul. He takes no salary and is always raising funds to give the students what they need to be successful—from PCs to gift cards to coaching calls. With an 85 percent college graduation rate, Jimmy has illuminated the path for hundreds of people.

It excites me to see one person's idea open future doors for so many.

Who inspires you?

_____

_____

How have your guides encouraged you along the way?

_____

_____

Were you ready for the messages, insights, resources, or tools they shared with you?

_____

_____

How are you using your money to extend your impact?

_____

_____

What groups do you invest in that bring you joy?

_____

_____

Who can you guide?

_____

_____

Key Finding #42

May your heart feel full for those who have helped you or those you have guided along the way.

CHAPTER 28

UNPACKING YOUR DECISIONS

I have learned that life is about opening doors, which can create different opportunities and pathways. Our commitments and how we align our time and funds create those pathways. I picked a computer information degree because I saw a college degree as a door opener that could lead to a better place. I was told during orientation that every student was hired out of the program. At the time, I did not necessarily like computers or telephone systems, but after years of earning minimum wage, I wanted a good-paying job. When I was assured that a four-year degree in computers would land me a decent salary, I signed up. I was uncertain in my abilities and fearful I would fail, but I was also determined to move beyond my current pay rate.

Even though the catalyst for a better salary drove me toward a career in technology, I am lucky, as I found the work interesting and enjoyed the fast pace and ever-changing environment. However, I cannot really tell you what I would have selected as a degree if my lack of finances was not driving my decision.

Money may or may not be a focal point for you, yet I have found that money is a hurdle that many women list as a reason they are not leaping into work that inspires them. Maybe there are other factors in your life that show up as obstacles, such as family approval, fear of failure, or low self-worth. Whatever may be holding you back from stepping into experiences or desires is worth exploring.

After hearing the stories of thousands of women I have met along my path, I believe that most of us have fears that lead to external dependencies. These dependencies then create internal struggles that shackle us to decisions and situations that prevent us from unleashing our life's work. We hold on to relationships, jobs, and situations that dim our light. I did this at different points in my life, so I am fully aware of how this "stuck" feeling can hinder progress. It often made me feel like my dreams were not possible, which overshadowed my most authentic self.

How have you seen money impact your decisions?

_____

_____

What drives most of your decisions?

_____

_____

What has you stuck right now?

_____

_____

Do you have other things nagging at you right now?

_____

_____

Here are more obstacles women have shared with me:

- "I am not ready."
- "My significant other thinks it is a bad idea."
- "My mother told me it was ridiculous."
- "I do not have the training."
- "I do not have enough time."
- "I cannot make it happen."

What would you add?

_____

_____

What is really holding you back?

_____

_____

Money has been a key lesson in my life and likely is the reason I was born into a household with very little of it. Much of my seeking has taught me that the parents we pick and the related situations inside our upbringings hold some of our most important life lessons. Crazy, I know, but it seems to be true for me. How about you?'

Key Finding #43

What doors are you opening or closing based on what you have learned or experienced as a child.

If people pick their parents, why do you think you picked yours?

_____

_____

What came forward about your childhood after reading this chapter?

_____

_____

What from your childhood defines you now?

_____

_____

What stories are still running your life?

_____

_____

Is it time to investigate beliefs that may be impacting your self-worth?

_____

_____

It is not always easy to unpack these life experiences, intersections where we have been guided, and stories we have collected along the way, yet many of them provide great insight and new levels of awareness. At this point of my journey, I made more time to invest in new levels of insight, including energy practices and practitioners that could help me dig deep into the buried stories that defined and impacted many of my decisions and actions.

This became a personal mission for me—one that started years ago with an acupressure tapping session that evolved into a journey of self-discovery to clear out what was no longer serving me. Why? Because I wanted to fill my inner areas of darkness with more light. I wanted to be filled with more joy and be aligned with gratitude, and I yearned for experiences and connections that created meaningful impact.

Through each session, learning, and lesson, I was building a toolkit of activities that helped me identify energy, where it was sitting, and its source. With this, I could decide what was serving my journey and what needed to be released.

Money, salary, and titles are defined and designed by humans to organize our existence. Is it right? Is it needed? I am not sure, but these external metrics often confuse our sense of self-worth, which impedes our life's work.

Now, years later, I am much better equipped to foster the momentum I need from within, rather than resorting to the external chase or perpetual avoidance based on believing that I am not good enough. But I had to learn how to unlearn my decades-long behaviors. What I have come to understand is that the reason we have chosen to come down to Earth is to learn, expand, and stretch beyond our egos and the limitations they create.

What behaviors do you need to unlearn?

_____

_____

What success metrics were defined early on that warrant further investigation?

_____

_____

What is driving you to seek?

_____

_____

What barriers have you created through your life experiences?

_____

_____

In what areas do you need to be more honest about how you set up your life?

_____

_____

What is holding you back now more than ever?

_____

_____

What do you have to investigate from your past that has a hold on your future?

_____

_____

It's not easy to unpack your life experiences and guided moments, the lessons you have learned from your parents, and the stories that guide your decisions. But, if you make the time to do so, you will find greater insights and new levels of awareness that will help you better align with your life's work. By valuing yourself by what you create energetically within and around you, you can shift your self-defined beliefs from fear of not having enough to a life of abundance and gratitude for all that crosses your path.

Key Finding #44

Identifying what is holding you back can be the key to open the doors you desire to walk through next.

CHAPTER 29

SELF-WORTH ANCHORED IN EXTERNAL METRICS

When I embarked on a path to seek more self-awareness and a deeper connection with myself, I had no idea of the hard facts I would have to learn about myself, my beliefs, and my perceived self-worth. When I started, the hard part was making the necessary shifts in my life and work while still accommodating the other loves of my life—my two kids, my husband, my friends, and various women's gatherings.

Although it took just about a year from my solo trip to Sedona, Arizona, to shift from my corporate role, it took many years to move beyond my perceived identity. I now know that while I was not prepared for the leap, I was strongly called to pursue researching, speaking, and writing so I could share strategies to help other women raise their frequencies and align with their life's work. With fear and lots of self-doubt, I leaped, reassuring myself that I could always go back.

I realize that not all women or men have the support they need from family and friends to take their own leaps. Even Sheryl Sandburg, author, woman in tech, billionaire, and philanthropist, talks about the importance of your life mate's support for your goals. Luckily, the mate I married, at age thirty, was on board with me selling my company stock and leaving my tech career to become an entrepreneur with a mission.

I think he believed that getting me off the road and out of the constant stress of a high-flying tech company would be a plus for our family and our relationship.

Little did he know, I thrived on the stress, the job, the title, and the pressure. So much so that I had no idea how much it defined me, and my self-perceived value, and frankly how much I liked myself until I left my corporate job.

You read that right; I aligned my self-worth with career-based milestones. Yes, I love my family and adore my kids, but I did not judge myself on my domestic outputs, which I could have if that was where I had spent the majority of my days. For me, at the time, I was at work for many hours a day, depending on the week. I am sure some of my readers can relate and some of them will have opinions, but regardless, that was my reality, and that is what I used to determine my self-worth.

I feel ridiculous sharing this truth, as I had hoped I was more grounded at that time. Yet my reality was that my ego was running my show. With this shift, I needed more from my husband—more recognition and more support, as I was used to a certain level of validation that I had left behind with my job. Through this transition, I struggled and at times I was depressed, leaning on my friends and husband for more of my self-worth.

It took years before I recognized that my decisions were being driven by fear and even longer before I discovered glimpses of my Soul shining through, providing me with more inner guidance. With this new insight, I must continue to keep daily tabs on my ego. If I overlook it, it will appear with self-doubt, worry, and anxiety.

Have you struggled with self-worth?

_____

_____

Do you align your value or self-worth with external metrics like your job, house, car, or relationship?

_____

_____

What stories have you carried with you for years that define your self-worth now?

_____

_____

Have you lost a job or a relationship that made you reflect on how that defined you?

_____

_____

Have you left the workforce and now doubt that you can get back in?

_____

_____

What do you do to stop the stories in your head from defining your self-worth, joy, and impact?

_____

_____

Many of you have already realized, through your own set of circumstances, what it took me four decades to admit to myself. I had allowed myself to be defined by outside metrics, which affected how I felt about myself.

Key Finding #45

Be aware of what fuels your self-worth.

PART III

UNCOVERING LIFE LESSONS

CHAPTER 30

THE REAL REASON I
VISITED A THERAPIST

I had no desire to dive into my childhood experiences, discuss my relationship with my sibling, or make correlations between my parents' marriage and mine. And I definitely did not want to discuss my dyslexia or obsessive-compulsive disorder (OCD).

With this, I strategically decided to lead my therapist Jill down an alternative path. I told her my main concern was that I needed to find more joy. I was not lying, as that was one of the results I was seeking, but it was not the catalyst.

The desire for more joy did not just appear one morning. My desire for more purpose and alignment had been an underlying desire for decades, yet I had skillfully ignored it by focusing on intense work, demanding schedules, and a need to excel. None of those things directly landed me in the therapist chair.

My dad was sick, I was waffling in my work, and a crack in my marriage appeared. I was doubting my abilities, scared of being alone, questioning my commitments, and fearful of everything crumbling. This was the catalyst that drove me to seek more help on my journey toward greater self-acceptance and self-love.

Such a series of events could be symbolized by the Tower card in a tarot deck, a collection of cards that are often used as a tool for spiritual guidance. The card represents a sizable situation with a graphical view of a Tower crumbling due to a lightning strike or other external forces. This card symbolized how I felt during that first visit with Jill when I accelerated my seeking based on my need to weather my own storm.

Now many may say the Tower card represents all or most things turning into crap, but others see this as the necessary end of one thing to make room for something else. At the time I would not have perceived my life needing a Tower moment, but now it is very evident that it was necessary.

If I was truly honest, this catalyst was not a complete surprise, as most spiritual books will share that the people close to us are often the most instrumental teachers. They bring forward essential experiences, specifically for us, that our Souls are here to learn. Because of my hours spent reading and listening to many spiritual authors, I had learned that the imbalances in our lives start and end with us.

Take, for example, those quotes or articles offering advice for a happy marriage or how to pick the right partner. Many share that you cannot successfully find in a partner what you don't already feel about yourself.

I was a perfect example of a person who felt accomplished, yet I was not my biggest fan. I would constantly listen to the voices in my mind that would scare, shame, and degrade my abilities and potential impact. I would freely give over my power to the nagging naysayer in my head, which I later learned was my ego. In doing so, my ego would often cripple my ability to believe I was enough.

Was I worth loving? I wanted my husband to acknowledge, see, and love all things in me, but did I see, love, and acknowledge myself? The sad truth was, I did not.

I would be lying if I said that I just decided to drive thousands of miles, read more than a hundred books, and meet with numerous Energy Practitioners and Lightworkers just because I desired more joy. I share in this book the more vulnerable side of my life, because without my awareness of my shortcomings, it would have been hard to move forward with the additional lessons—they would never have happened without the feelings of loneliness, fear, disappointment, and sadness. These emotions created my desire to shift, which was an essential piece of why I committed to my seeking. I had to get to the bottom of who I was and what I needed before I could like myself without any external metrics. This was the basis for my journey of awakening that led me to tackle my lessons, which uncovered these findings that guided me toward more energy and alignment with my life's work.

For some of us, these lessons show up in our relationship with the most significant person in our lives.

Gary Zukav, the author of *Seat of the Soul*, enlightened me about the teaching of a Soul mate, which was so beautifully captured in *Mosaic's* Interview with Gary Zukav and Linda Francis, July 9, 2008 – Issue 44, Fall 2008. The publication has since been retired, but most of their work can be found at the Seat of the Soul Institute, and the link can be found in Appendix A.

*"**Gary:** The purpose of relationships from a spiritual perspective is to grow spiritually and that means to become someone who is more emotionally aware, more able to choose responsibly, more able to consult intuition, more able to use his or her experiences, including the most painful experiences, in order to create a life of meaning and joy and purpose and fulfillment. A spiritual partnership specifically is a partnership between equals for the purpose of spiritual growth."*

Before discovering Gary's work, I didn't recognize that the relationships I picked were essentially aligned with lessons I was ready to learn. I met and dated many wonderful people, and some not so wonderful people. As I reflect on those connections, most had shown me more about myself.

Many of relationships before my husband were short-lived. As I reflect on the challenges each relationship presented, I realize that at the time, working through the obstacles seemed unnecessary, which is likely why it did not work out or one of us chose to move on.

Who in your life is activating your lessons?

_____

_____

Who in your life is hindering your growth?

_____

_____

Who in your life do you see as an equal, for the purpose of spiritual growth?

_____

_____

During the first decade of my marriage, I am not sure I would have described our relationship as a spiritual partnership. We, like many marriages, worked through many firsts. First house, first dog, first kid, first loss, and so on. Along the way, and at different times, each of us has chosen to take the lead or love a little more as the other worked through life lessons.

Throughout the years, we have been tested and at times forced to reevaluate and reprioritize our commitment to each other. For anyone who has been married or committed for decades, it is not easy to keep things going in the right direction while evolving yourself, your family, and your relationship with each other. I think people with long term-relationships will agree that each couple needs to define what partnership means to them while delicately balancing their interpretations and related actions associated with love. Some couples will find themselves inside a spiritual partnership, and other couples will not, as our work within ourselves will determine the type of relationship we attract externally and the level of growth and connection we receive.

For our partnership, it has taken many life decisions, such as how we chose to spend our time, what information we consume, and how we prioritize and support each other. Looking back on those choices, we have agreed to seek our truth and create a more committed and meaningful relationship with both ourselves and each other. We have both taken the time over the years to do the self-discovery, which created new levels of self-awareness and eventually a greater level of appreciation for each other. After many years and some notable ups and downs, we have moved beyond where we started and expanded into a spiritual partnership.

I am not suggesting this should be your path or that I have any idea what next week will bring, as our lives are unpredictable. The reassurance that sets my mind at ease is that your journey is spiritually created just for you. How you will respond and how you will address your behavior, engagement, and interactions is up to you. When it seems like it's too much or you feel stuck, find a guide or expert to help you work through your lessons.

There are many podcasts, books, meditations, retreats, and energy practices to guide and help. Or if you are not up for the research, tap into the Energy Practitioners and Lightworkers I have worked with inside my community.

Alicia Thompson was one of my guides during a desperate time. My Tower was falling, and I needed to explore deeper questions, find more meaning, and gain new perspectives on how I viewed myself and my choices.

This time instead of blaming, I was working to understand my reactions and the stories brewing in my head. I remembered listening to a book years earlier that shared how when we point our finger at others, our other fingers are pointing back at us, which was a good reminder that I had to work on myself before I expected things to shift.

Sifting through my notes, I stumbled upon *The Work* of Byron Katie, which is what led me to this beautiful Lightworker, Alicia. She met me online and, on numerous occasions, guided my thoughts, responses, and feelings. Through the four specific questions designed by Byron, Alicia helped me find some peace within my circumstances.

As a Certified Clarity Coach, Alicia utilized meditative strategies to help me identify conditioning that caused my sense of victimhood, self-doubt, limited thinking, anxiety, and worry. Her work helped me recognize the patterns, conditions, and beliefs around my thoughts, which held the keys to some of my life lessons. Her practices and coaching practices shined a light on the difference between the common misconception that life happens to us versus accepting and knowing the spiritual truth that life happens *for* us.

I am not sure how I would have handled my despair during this Tower card situation had I not had Lightworkers in my life. They shared love and reassurance when I felt so alone and too embarrassed to share the events in my life with some of my friends and family. I am truly grateful to the women who shined their lights on me when I felt so gloomy and sad.

You will continue to find that I lean on many women who share their knowing and energy practices with me when I am seeking to remove the darkness and raise my frequency. I will continue to reveal the many Lightworkers, spiritual seekers, and healers I have worked with along the way to help me through my process of uncovering my gifts, work, and alignment. You can connect with many of them directly inside www.TogetherWeSeek.Online, including Alicia, and be sure to check out her interview too where she shares her Tower moment that has brought her to more self-acceptance and love.

If you are ready to dig through more of your stories to release stuck energy, let's keep excavating!

 ### *Key Finding #46*

All your relationships are spiritual. There is a purpose for each one of them.

CHAPTER 31

DID WE PICK OUR MOTHERS?

The range of emotions we feel about our mothers can be broad. The stories can be lengthy and complex. The feelings that we have are real, spanning from love to disconnect to admiration to frustration to anger to appreciation to ambivalence or some combination of feelings.

I think it is safe to say that the energies between the Souls of mothers and daughters are often not simple or predictable. And the energetic bond I have with my own mother is no exception. However, I certainly did not expect the energy of my mother to surface in Irwin, Pennsylvania.

My session ended, or so I thought. As I was putting my shoes on and digging through my bag for payment, I could feel a wave of nausea coming on fast, and I think Paula could tell by the look on my face. She quickly stood up and shepherded me back to her table. I could feel her hand guide me as I lay back down.

Her massage table was a familiar place. I had already been there for more than an hour, and this was likely my seventh visit. I traveled back and forth every other week between the bookends of my children's school bus pickups and drop offs. As the bus carried off my kids, I would hurry back to the house, pack my car, and start my two-hour journey to Irwin to visit Paula Marzaloes just outside Pittsburgh.

My initial goal for my visits was to help shift some of my energy, as it was wreaking havoc on my internal stories and negatively impacting my joy. I often call this dark energy.

During my first few visits, it was apparent that Paula was a gifted healer. On this specific day, it was clear to her, and now me, that I needed more time, as I had some energy that was ready to be released. I expected to lie alone on that familiar table, allowing my body to recalibrate, but Paula did not leave my side. She continued to work with my body, assessing my energy flow with her hand as she worked to identify the source.

Quickly narrowing down the time frame, she was able to pinpoint the event that has had a grip on me for decades, and maybe lifetimes. Through a series of questions, she focused on my relationship with my mother. My connection with my mother was much more profound than met the eye.

Through girlfriends and professional connections, I have found that most women have strong feelings when it comes to their mothers. My feelings also span the spectrum, which scares me, as I am raising a daughter of my own.

As many of us mothers know, it takes a lot of patience, self-awareness, and self-acceptance to guide and nurture children. We do not always get it right, and the thought of not being strongly connected to my daughter later in life saddens me.

It is not that the women I know do not love their mothers, but there is often some unsettled business between them. And sometimes, it does not even make sense why this unsettled feeling exists, as if the energy between them lingers from another time or situation. And it's as if we had a previous experience or series of situations that amplified the energy we now feel around our mothers.

This reminds me of a time when my son was about three years old. We were in his room one evening, on the floor playing with his train. He looked me straight in the eyes and said, "I knew you before I came here." I was taken aback by his words and tried to get him to elaborate, but he continued to play on his train table as if he had just shared an ordinary detail about his day.

Did our kids know us or our Souls before they arrived, and did we have a previous experience with or pick our mothers for a reason? Does your mother have a Soul lesson for you?

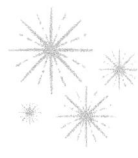 **Key Finding #47**

Your Soul's knowing may span beyond your current experiences.

CHAPTER 32

OUR MOTHERS COME
WITH SOUL LESSONS

I love my mom and am grateful for her love and guidance, but there was more to us—an energy that I had known for years but honestly could not make sense of until that specific session with Paula. As I was lying on the table, I seemed to be going in and out of an altered state of consciousness because I started seeing visions and colors.

Our mothers often bring forward many of our life lessons. Some of these are highlighted in commercials, movies, and other media, but I am referring to a deeper experience. We share an energetic connection with them that represents lessons our Souls have experienced before, yet these lessons are difficult to quantify. I needed the help of Energy Practitioners to make sense of some of these feelings, lessons, and connections.

What I have learned through the help of many Energy Practitioners is that my mother, in a nutshell, represents my inability to break free. Even after decades of experiencing this firsthand, it still hurts my heart and, at times, brings tears to my eyes. I want nothing more than for her to spread her wings and trust her knowing to step into her dreams.

I will sidestep the sappiness and cut to the chase; my mother was one of my more instrumental Soul lessons. I am going to take a leap and suggest that this is the case for many women. My husband and kids are also in that grouping, as they are the closest Souls to me.

A *Soul lesson* is something we are here to learn. It could be magical, or difficult, or something in between. In any case, your Soul is here to experience, stretch, learn, love, and grow. For many of us, our relationships bring these lessons to the forefront. For many women, the mother-daughter lesson is instrumental and can vary by child. This was taught by Molly C. Gauthier, who points out that your astrological moon sign at birth represents the energy that your mother brings into your life.

Mothers bear the load of many on their journeys. And now that I am a mother, I am experiencing this firsthand, which gives me so much appreciation for my mother and all mothers. Being a mother means many things. You could mother your nuclear family, students, animals, a product or solution to be shared, or anything that needs support, love, empowerment, and guidance. We often get caught up on society's associations or terminology, but no need; you know inherently if you are or have been mothering something.

Thinking about your mother as you work through these questions, know that there is no judgment. And if your mother is not the best person for these questions, feel free to replace the word "mother" with a person who is instrumental in your life. These questions are designed to help you find the stories that are holding you back from sharing your gifts with the world.

How much love and connection do you feel with your mother?

_____

_____

What is your biggest rub with your mother?

_____

_____

How does/did she support you?

_____

_____

How does/did she frustrate you?

_____

_____

What does/did she do that you promised yourself you would never do?

_____

_____

What bugs you about yourself that you see/saw in your mother?

_____

_____

What do/did you see in your mother that you have worked so hard to avoid?

_____

_____

What important lesson or lessons do you think your mother is here to teach you?

_____

_____

How do/did you support your mother?

_____

_____

Let me assure you that your mother is not your mother by accident. My spiritual teachers taught me that I chose my parents, which surprised me at first. My son also shared an instrumental nugget in this realization—he may have known me before he arrived here. The fact that he told me this still fascinates me!

Now some of you may be feeling a touch of nausea like I did with Paula. Some of you may feel happy, sad, relieved, or some other emotion. You may want to take the time to journal more deeply on a few of these questions and the emotions that come up.

As I mentioned above, you can go through these questions and replace your mother with a father, aunt, uncle, sister, brother, or any other person you grew up with who influenced how you feel about yourself. You can even use it for people in your life today that you didn't grow up with, such as a partner or close friend.

I do or do not believe I picked my mother because:

_____

_____

If I did pick my mother, it makes me feel:

_____

_____

I cherish or appreciate my mother because:

_____

_____

I have already learned this from my mother:

_____

_____

Could it be that our mothers are here for guidance, and maybe love, but most of all, to empower us to learn, shift, or get a glimpse of our life's work? While this concept is profound for some women and abstract for others, my findings to date have pointed me to such a glimpse.

This might not resonate with you right now, but stick with me and be sure to answer or even journal about the questions above.

Key Finding #48

We have chosen certain relationships because of the lessons these people offer us for our growth.

CHAPTER 33

RELEASING THE INTERDEPENDENCIES

After meditation, prayer, and a series of hand movements, Paula placed three crystals in my hand and then left the room. Before she left, she encouraged me to let my mind wander and be a witness to the experience. My five senses were activated by the smell of her beautiful oils, the mist of a small office waterfall, and the sound of meditative music. My mind was relaxed, and my thoughts became fluid.

The visualization appeared almost immediately. It was surprising yet beautiful. Two spheres of colors appeared and looked very much interconnected. As I observed them, seemingly from afar, I could feel my mother's love and willingness to help. I could also sense her familiar fears, disappointment, and struggles.

As I allowed myself to feel her energy, I could feel her vibration in close proximity. With a tugging sensation around my heart, my chest felt heavy, and I found myself energetically near my mother even though she was physically hundreds of miles away.

The connection between her sphere and mine seemed intertwined, with little separation. It did not make sense to me because at times I have felt so different and disconnected from my mother.

However, even though it was unfamiliar to my mind, our vibrational link seemed very connected. It almost seemed like we were one, yet I felt so separated. I took physical notice of my desire not to be connected in that way.

A feeling of guilt rushed through my body. I love my mom, but I asked, "Why are our energy fields so undeniably intertwined?" The answer came in just as quickly as the guilt. I could feel with all my senses that our two Souls had an interdependency well before we came together here. Our Souls were tethered in a way that kept my mom in her safe place and me from feeling as though my work was incomplete, as I still could not help her find her way.

My training ground for working with women started years before I questioned the man in the retail store. The basis of my work had begun at home, watching my mother give up her dreams time and time again to obey the Souls around her. It began when she was young, with abusive parents, and continued when she picked her mate. Worn down from her relationships and her loved ones' needs to control her, she lost sight of her inner spark that once had fueled her dreams.

My controlling grandmother impacted my mother's opportunities, friendships, and experiences because of her fear of uncomfortable situations, including whippings, groundings, and verbal abuse. Trained to obey as a young girl and eager to get out of the house, she landed in the arms of my dad, who was an unsophisticated, fear-based Soul who acted more like a toddler than a grown man.

Like most kids, I too sought love from my parents, which included my dad. I now believe he loved me as much as he knew how. I am grateful that he was not nearly as much of a bully with me as he was with my mom, as I think his Soul knew that I was fierce inside, even when I was young.

It was heart-wrenching at times to watch their exchanges. I am sure neither one of them was ever very happy in the marriage. Frankly, they should have separated decades earlier, but both were too afraid of the unknown.

As Gary Zukav, author of *The Seat of The Soul*, highlights, and I am paraphrasing, even though humans have developed the tradition of marriage, our Souls are on a journey that does not align with these human rules.

As an adult observing my parents, I now find myself encouraging my mother to get out, make her way, and get going on her dreams. Although it appeared that she could muster up enough courage, it never happened. My parents recently reached their fiftieth wedding anniversary, but it came and went with not much to celebrate outside of going to dinner.

Little did I know that watching my mom's Soul journey was part of my life's work and my Soul's journey. Much of the work I do now—to encourage women to get out from what is holding them down or back—I do because of what I saw while growing up in my household.

My mom has said on numerous occasions that it was important to give her kids the love she did not feel. She did this by giving up her dreams to help make our dreams a reality. I am not certain this was necessary, but I think it helps her accept her choices.

What is coming forward for you? What are you thinking about from your childhood?

_____

_____

What did you experience as a child that may give you insight into your Soul's lessons or life's work?

_____

_____

What did you see happen to your mom or dad or family member that frustrated you?

_____

_____

It would hurt my heart if I jumped ahead without mentioning that I am grateful for my mom and dad. They both have good hearts, even though they were often hidden behind disappointed faces. They could have easily tarnished or even wrecked our Souls, as some parents do to their children. I am at peace with the energy I have with both my parents, as they supported and celebrated us, and for that, I am so grateful.

There are many paths, and some Souls experience levels of disappointment, betrayal, and abuse beyond what is imaginable. If this is you, I am sorry. It is not fair, and it does not always make sense, but you are in control of how you move through your life as an adult. There are many Energy Practitioners who can help you clear out the old or even dark energy to create space for more light and love.

Perhaps you are recognizing that now, as an adult, you are repeating some situations from your childhood. This is quite common. Many of us repeat comparable situations with different people who have similar characteristics to our family members. These people show up in our lives with different physical features, costumes, and backgrounds, yet they play similar roles so we can continue to learn our Soul lessons.

What lesson or lessons do you have on repeat?

_____

_____

What is the characteristic or trait of the people helping you learn this lesson?

_____

_____

What is difficult about this lesson for you?

_____

_____

What is your heart calling you to do?

_____

_____

Do you need to give yourself permission to pick yourself?

_____

_____

Is it time for you to make room to clear out what is no longer useful in your life?

_____

_____

Sometimes it is not always obvious that situations are happening *for* us. Take some time to think about the areas of your life that need some more in-depth evaluation to identify the lessons the Universe is trying to teach you.

It still makes me sad that my mom missed some opportunities to stand up to those bullying Souls. After my many therapy and energy sessions, I now understand that it is her choice to step in or push away from her life lessons. Her Soul has found ways to sustain a manageable frequency—likely not the one she desires but the one she can live within. I hope she still has time to prioritize herself through self-love and self-acceptance.

As I lay there, I realized this was likely a defining moment in Paula's office. During my visualization, the crystals in my hand seemed to create a crystal bridge. The bright light from beyond made its way over to our spheres and shined upon us. The knowing in the light encouraged my mother and me to let go and move independently yet on parallel paths into our own Soul spheres (the individual energy bubbles in which all humans reside).

Her Soul was resistant at first because she found comfort, connection, and liberation in my Soul sphere. I could feel her fear. Looking back, I think she took on my energy, which made her feel full enough. I think it is likely that my frequency prevented her from stepping out in her own way to gain her life lessons.

I reassured her through my Soul field that the light of the Heavenly Mother would guide her. In an effort to separate our Souls' fields of energy, which I refer to as Soul spheres, I asked for Archangel Michael and all the angels to help remove the cords that were no longer serving us in a positive way.

Cords are essentially energy strands between two entities. You can de-cord these strands, which are attached to both of your bodies, at any time. This knowledge that

I could ask Archangel Michael to remove the cords was a gift I had learned years earlier in Sedona with Angel Guide Stacey Alexander.

As our spheres of light separated with the help of the energy of many angels, I could feel how tightly corded we were to one another. As we worked to unravel the cord that wrapped us so deeply together, I could feel a release of energy near and around my heart. I called on the angels once again to sprinkle healing waters from the Creator into the gaping hole to clean and mend our hearts so we could both be open to new levels of light and love.

With a few strands left to untwist, I recognized the need for my mother to let go. I reached her ears with a kind and loving voice, reassuring her that she could stand alone and she could find the peace she yearned for this time around. With the help from the Universal Mother, she tearfully yet joyfully released the remaining threads of the cord.

The angels that assisted Archangel Michael kept busy cleaning and healing as tears flowed down my face. I physically felt the release and light energy in my chest and around my heart, and I visually watched my mother's Soul sphere rise beside me. As parallel spheres with golden light from above, we were blessed. As I took a deep breath, I felt relieved, joyful, and excited now that we were vibrating on parallel planes.

I was then escorted back to my physical state. Paula returned, my nausea was gone, and I once again put on my shoes.

The experience felt profound. Even though my mother was hundreds of miles from me, our Souls were doing work beyond our physical state and in the Universal Light. As I look back, I realize that all the spiritual work I had done before that date had prepared me for that powerful release.

My relationship with my mother had been evolving. I had to let go of her and she me. Even though I have never spoken of that day with her, I have seen her step forward in situations where she used to hold back.

If your relationships have you stuck in holding patterns preventing you from reaching the levels of enlightenment, energy, or experiences you desire, you can change your dependencies, alignment, or internal stories.

What is coming up for you now?

_____

_____

What relationships seem to have an energy that seeps into your sphere?

_____

_____

What are you carrying that is not yours?

_____

_____

What is in your Soul sphere that you are ready to release?

_____

_____

I can assure you that Lightworkers and Energy Practitioners are all around us. To make it easy for you to get acquainted with the various practices and practitioners in a safe place, I have brought together many incredible women who have helped me create more space for love and light. You can find many of them at www. TogetherWeSeek.Online.

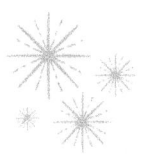 ### *Key Finding #49*

You can change, at any time, the dynamics of relationships that are holding you back.

CHAPTER 34

RECOGNIZING THE ENERGY AROUND YOU

Relationships will come and go. Some will be joyful; others difficult. Some relationships will last a lifetime; others will be based on circumstances. The key to successfully learning from our relationships is knowing that they are instrumental in many of our life lessons and can even provide glimpses into our life's work.

The power of relationships to enlighten our journeys and Souls was highlighted by Gary Zukav, author of *The Seat of the Soul*. Gary writes that some of our closest relationships create insights into our life's lessons. The way he shares his message encourages me to view my experiences and relationships through a different lens. Gary's lessons shifted my view so I could consider how my relationships, situations, and events were happening for me rather than to me, with the purpose of balancing and evolving the energy of my Soul.

The lessons may not make sense at first, but many of us can look back at a situation, relationship, or series of events and find our lessons and potentially gain a glimpse of our life's work.

It was not until recently that I recognized different patterns in my relationships and even events that have pushed me to grow and expand beyond my current comfort zone. Then other relationships provided tests to see if I had learned to set healthy boundaries. And other occurrences with people have left me questioning how I showed up and even responded.

I must admit that when I was single, I did not know how to date. I fumbled, often, and many of my actions back then make me cringe now. I realize that this is not a dating book, but I do think it is important to be curious about how we show up, especially in vulnerable situations, and remind ourselves that even our not-so-glamorous or even unhealthy relationships have their place in our lessons and growth.

As you now know, I grew up with a mom who was eager to stand in her light but was heavily discouraged by her circumstances. Unfortunately, she allowed others to make her choices for her, so she stayed small and quiet with the advice she shared and how she showed up for me. Now when I experience women in similar situations, I tend to tap into the energy of watching my mom for so many years. With this, I often react with bold actions as I did early in my life, such as when I went head-on with a stranger in a retail store who I thought was bullying a woman.

With a need to learn from more women who were ahead of me on their journeys, I created opportunities and communities for women to come together. Then I started writing down the stories I collected for me, my daughter, and any woman interested in overcoming the ridiculous pressure and expectations placed on us at home and at work, which some refer to as "having it all."

These activities catapulted me into conversations with women about how to pave our paths for our professional goals and desires, which I had previously believed was straightforward. Through my research, I learned that the masculine energy that acts as the underpinning at work is only half of the story. These new levels of awakening have once again brought me to the keyboard, as I have uncovered new findings that I feel are important to share with more women.

I see these messages, situations, and even exchanges as a series of breadcrumbs that started with people and relationships forming the bedrock of insights that began shining light onto my life's work.

What breadcrumbs have you noticed throughout your life?

_____

_____

What life moments, relationships, and milestones did not seem obvious until now?

_____

_____

What do you plan to consider and explore more of now?

_____

_____

Relationships are multi-faceted, and our interactions can trigger all types of emotions, including frustrations. We have no playbooks to manage our responses when other people behave in unhealthy, mean, or ugly ways.

If you have had to interact with people who carry very dark energy, I am sorry, as there are often no excuses for those who behave in unhealthy, mean, or ugly ways.

Recognizing these people in your life is key to moving beyond the negative energy. For years, I thought having people in my life who interacted with unhealthy behaviors was just how life was, and it happened to everybody. However, I have learned through my own research that my energy attracts similar energy. My frequency is like a radio station for all to hear and even feel. If I do not like the energy coming my way, I must assess and shift my energy first.

If you have spent years attracting unhealthy energy from others, then you, too, can make time to adjust your energy to create space for more love and light. It is not always easy but is often necessary if you are ready to shift your life into a healthier and higher frequency. As Byron Katie reminds us inside "Forgiveness Is Not What You Think—The Work of Byron Katie®," a video on YouTube, remembering our trauma hurts. Byron's work guides people through how to evaluate situations that bring up fear, doubt, denial, and rejection. These are often the experiences that leave us feeling beat up, unsettled, and even unloved.

I have encountered many practitioners who help heal trauma without requiring the client to go through the experience again. It can be done; I have worked through and healed traumatic past experiences with their wise guidance and comforting support.

In fact, I had an excellent TRE® session with Wendy Kimball while working on this chapter. TRE® or Trauma and Tension Release Exercises is an innovative series of exercises that assists the body in releasing deep muscular patterns of stress, tension, and trauma.

Through an online 90-minute video session, without requiring me to revisit any one story or life experience, Wendy graciously guided me through easy exercises that activate a natural reflex mechanism of shaking or vibrating that released muscular tension, calming down the nervous system. Almost immediately, I felt an energy release, which is still in effect today.

This is Wendy's second career. Filled with love and appreciation, Wendy now helps others on their journeys toward empowerment and healing, as she is passionate about teaching others to heal themselves from stress, tension, and trauma.

You can find my interview with Wendy highlighting her shift from a government job to this type of energy work in my community. Wendy, along with many practitioners, can create safe places to release energy no longer serving her clients.

As you seek new levels of self-enlightenment within your body and life to grow into more love and light, you are likely to encounter new relationships. Some will test you; others will lift you up. It is up to you to decide what frequency you want to live within, which is usually based on your level of gratitude, self-love, and acceptance. Your energy will drive your feelings and then your actions in your relationships.

Key Finding #50

Your relationships provide insight into where you are on your journey.

CHAPTER 35

OUR RELATIONSHIPS MIRROR OUR ENERGY

As I worked to brighten my light and shed the stories and feelings that had kept me in a holding pattern, I had to decide how I was going to handle relationships that were created when I was in a different band of frequency, or a different energy level.

When I was working to align with more love, appreciation, and gratitude, some relationships that I created at a time when I was more fearful and self-doubting came to an end. Some departed with ease, and others created a stinging effect. I have seen in many books and in my life that the Universe helps make space for what is next, especially if you are prioritizing self-discovery and making room for more light.

Sarah Steel confirmed this when she joined me to discuss "Past Life Regression – The Experience and Benefits." Her work helps her clients heal their pasts so they can live their purpose in the present. We met up for the *Together We Seek* podcast and she, too, said that some relationships essentially evaporated when she worked to raise her energy.

As you enhance or elevate your vibrational levels, you'll find that those with lower frequencies are usually not interested in being around those in higher bands. So don't take it personally. It is a sign you are leveling up your energy and your alignment.

Even with this knowledge, I still like to reflect on memories, experiences, and lessons I learned through my relationships. Think about a relationship in which you have encountered some hiccups or uncomfortable meetups or discussions and answer the following questions.

- What emotions does this relationship bring up? (Fear, self-doubt, unloveableness, aloneness, unacceptability)
- Will I care about this hiccup in one month, one year, or ten years?
- Why is this happening for me (rather than to me) now?
- Do I see the lesson within this relationship?
- Did I see this lesson coming?
- Is the lesson repeating itself in my life?
- What could I learn from this situation?
- How can I love myself right now?
- Do I have a new perspective about this relationship?
- Is it time for me to choose myself?
- Do I have to make different choices related to how I engage with this person?
- Is this a healthy relationship for me?
- What about my energy is attracting this energy?
- What would I tell a daughter or niece if she were in a similar situation?

As you continue to evolve and morph by doing more of your inside work, the lessons are more pronounced and sometimes give rise to more emotions. After listening to *The Universe Has Your Back: Transform Fear into Faith* by Gabrielle Bernstein, I asked the Universe to clear out the darkness and bring in more light. It soon became clear to me that my inner work to raise my frequency was underway. Little did I know that transformation was going to happen in all aspects of my life, including my relationships.

Key Finding # 51

Remember, how you respond is more about your teachings, growth, and enlightenment than it is about the other person.

Before I wrote the previous few chapters on relationships, I pulled two oracle cards from Kyle Gray's *Keeper of the Light*. The Mercury card said, "Get the weight off your chest," and the Myriam card said, "Choose to forgive."

After pulling this card, I recalled a friendship that slipped away. Our relationship had been showing up in new and different ways for more than a year. One day, during a heated conversation, it finally came to a head. The actions and comments we exchanged did not align with the friendship I thought I knew. I cried for weeks, as it created a painful separation between us. It felt like a breakup, and I found myself reviewing the exchange in detail. I tried to make sense of it, but when weeks became months and eventually a year, it became clear that our frequencies no longer aligned and the Universe was doing what it does best—ushering me along.

Even though I was aware of this, I still felt some lingering energy associated with this shift. The card I pulled gave me encouragement to flush out any areas in my body that were still holding that experience.

As I sat in my office, I visualized a cleaning that started at the top of my head, moved down my neck and throat, down my chest and torso, through my stomach, pelvis, and back. Then it went down my thighs, over my knees, through my calves, over my ankles, into my feet, down into the floor, and into the Earth. My friend, editor, and author of many books, including *Hidden Voices: Biblical Women and Our Christian Heritage*, Heidi Bright, shared that the darker energies get mulched by Mother Earth. This resonates with me, as I then think of all the beautiful flowers that grow in mulch. This movement of energy flowing out of my body into Mother Earth creates energetic space throughout my body where the light can shine and illuminate my path for what is next.

What is still lingering inside you?

_____

_____

What energy can you let go to act as mulch for Mother Earth?

_____

_____

What person came to mind during this chapter?

_____

_____

What relationships are you holding on to that need to be released?

_____

_____

Anyone who has done energy work knows you cannot always control the beams of your light. As you spend time clearing out the stories, dependencies, and even darkness, the light will emerge, which may not be immediately apparent. But trust me, if you work to clear out the dark energy and align with more gratitude for the things in your life, you will eventually encounter new people and experiences that align with your upgraded frequency.

Key Finding #52

Relationships are designed to enhance our learnings and ultimately our journeys.

CHAPTER 36

THREADS FROM OUR CHILDHOOD EXPERIENCES

Much of our lives is deeply influenced by our experiences, choices, and relationships, some starting back in our childhoods. This became clear to me when I began having energy sessions with Peggy Koelliker, a CPA and founder of The Healing Connection. Peggy provides simple, cutting-edge strategies to help her clients keep their energies flowing for optimum health, increased vitality, spiritual awareness, a peaceful mind, and deep relaxation.

Peggy became interested in the healing profession while teaching communication skills to business executives for a nationally recognized training center. She discovered for herself, and through her clients, the role of deep breathing in one's ability to relax. She also learned the importance of quieting the mind and listening to the intuitive voice within to become more effective on the job and in one's personal life.

This fascination with the body's self-healing mechanisms and the untapped powers of the mind led Peggy to obtain certifications in Eden Energy Medicine, emotional freedom technique (EFT), Usui and Karuna Reiki, and many more healing modalities. Check out her website, which I have included in Appendix A, for all the services Peggy has to offer.

During my first one-on-one visit with Peggy, which occurred after I attended her group mindfulness class, I was enthralled by her professional journey that evolved into spiritual practices and eventually a business. I had so many questions for her until she stopped me and said, "JJ, why are you here?"

Yikes. I did not want to speak my truth. I wanted to mislead her like I did my previous therapists.

Of course, I wanted help, but I did not want to be vulnerable. I did not want to share any stories that would show that I did not have it together or that I had failed.

My mind raced. *What do I say? Don't tell her the truth. Time to go!*

I smiled and could feel a tear on my cheek. Out of desperation, I said as quickly as I could, "I am ready to work on my marriage."

This might seem odd, as I was there alone, but I felt that I needed to get underneath my stories, as I was holding back—though in a different way than my spouse. My holding back was my fear of leaning in. As I mentioned before, our closest relationships bring forward our biggest lessons.

Relieved by my courage to finally speak my truth and be transparent, I felt ready to dive into some personal energy clearing with Peggy. What I was not expecting was for her to intuitively take me down a path that unraveled some of my parents' relationship patterns and how I had brought them forward into my own marriage.

Stomaching this truth brought up painful emotions for me. That one tear turned into many, as my parents' relationship has some unhealthy patterns. Deep down, I feared my mom's truth of losing herself in her choices and fearful that I should have listened to her words and bypassed marriage. I had grown up watching her give up many of her dreams to please my dad. At the core, I believe my dad is insecure and therefore micromanages my mom and her actions. He, of course, would never admit this, but I have done enough self-work to see the root of his actions. His demands of her to stay close to our home outside of the time she spent at work were rooted in a fear that she might wander off or meet another man. These demands fueled some of their fights and eventually created a housebound wife.

With this, my mom encouraged me from a young age not to marry. As a result, I often had a hard time committing to a relationship. Even when I met my husband. He could not have been more different than my dad, but it took years for me to settle in, as I often reflected on the dynamics of my parents' marriage and my mother's warnings.

On numerous occasions, I have shared with my mom that part of her life's work is breaking through the barriers others created for her. I have even suggested small steps she can take to build momentum and gain the confidence she needs to trust in herself and her actions so she can step into what she wants in this life. Never did I think I had to follow my own advice and work on stepping into the life I wanted.

As her daughter, I find it difficult to watch her lose sight of her dreams. Occasionally, I can see a glimmer in her eyes, but it quickly fades with her perceived reality and the tiredness of her body. I know now that I, too, was afraid of running out of time, which is why I spend so many hours working on projects that are important to me and my Soul.

I want nothing more than for my mom, and every woman, to break free of the overshadowing energy that holds her back. With this, I have tried to be an inspiration to her through my actions, gifts, and support. I have even tried to book her sessions with Lightworkers and coaches to create what her heart desires, but her relationships, upbringing, and path created an overwhelming sense of fear and defeat that wore her down before she learned how to illuminate her path.

Soon I realized that I needed to book some of these energy sessions for myself, as I was losing myself in my own stories, some of which were created when I was a child. I also had to recognize that my mother's relationship with my father is one of her lessons. I witnessed it and created many stories that I have since worked to unravel, but I had to separate out my energy sphere from my mother's and from the feelings I had about my father based on their exchanges.

This unraveling is not easy, but over the years, it has allowed me to see my dad independently. Before, my emotions and my perception of my dad were engulfed in my mom's emotions around their relationship. I can now say that I have a love for my dad. He was not emotionally available, but he was proud and supportive. He struggled with an enormous amount of fear and self-doubt that impacted his confidence, which was evident in his marriage. His insecurities and fear took the lead, and as a result, he micromanaged the people who allowed him to do so.

My mom, in despair, turned her focus onto us kids and our journeys. She successfully broke the cycle of child abuse that ran rampant in her past. I know it was not easy at times, but she poured every ounce of love into us that she wished she had been given. She shared small inspirations such as a cup of tea, the smell of a newly picked flower, or unexpected tickle time. Her commitment to us was undeniable as she consciously guided us away from the pitfalls she had encountered while growing up. In doing so, she urged me not to settle, settle down, or marry, which fueled much of my determination and drive. Yet this message took some time for me to untangle, which I did not realize I needed to do until I was sitting with Peggy.

What programming did you receive from an early age?

_____

_____

What stories do you reference from your upbringing?

_____

_____

What patterns do you carry into your relationships that you were exposed to as a child?

_____

_____

Although my parents struggled on many levels, they did praise my brother and me for our hard work. Because they struggled financially, we were encouraged to contribute at an early age. My parents' appreciation and praise grew as I moved from pool cleaner to baker to waitress, helping to provide for our household. These early external approvals were noted by my ego and likely drove the internal stories that kept me chasing professional milestones and accolades, working late nights and feeding my competitive nature.

What external metrics are you striving for because of your upbringing?

_____

_____

How do you see these experiences and stories showing up in your life now?

_____

_____

What are you ready to release?

_____

_____

I never expected when I hit a rough patch in my marriage that I would be sitting with an EFT practitioner talking through my parents' relationship. In fact, many of the energy practices I share here and ahead were instrumental, as their assistance guided me through experiences and tools I used to dive into some of the stories and self-doubt hurdles.

I am not the poster woman for leaving your day job to pursue your passions full time. But for me, it was the rattling of the cage that stripped me of my security blanket, as I defined myself by work. This was instrumental in my life, as it forced me to seek, to figure out who I really was, what made me tick, and essentially bring me to the work I am doing right now.

We all have our paths, so I am not suggesting that it's necessary for you to leave your job to raise your frequency or align with your life's work. Many do this off the sides of their desks or during the evenings or weekends, as their jobs provide the means or structure they need for everything in their life to work.

I was not expecting to disclose so much about my family dynamics when I decided to write this book, but it is necessary for me to share how this seeking started and how I encountered all these amazing people who have helped me dig through my stories and align with my life's work.

I hope these stories give you insight into why things may be happening now in your life that you do or do not understand. Your experiences, decisions, and family dynamics likely provide some key insights into your patterns, your stories, and your journey.

Key Finding #53

Our childhood difficulties often give us clues into energy we carry into future relationships.

PART IV

GETTING PRESENT WITH MINDFULNESS

CHAPTER 37

THE LURKING ENERGIES THAT INFUSE OUR SELF-WORTH

Once I stripped myself of my title, salary, and the prestige of working in Silicon Valley, it took me years to rediscover my identity, self-worth, and perceived value, as many of my self-worth stories started when I was a kid. I initially felt foolish about moving into the self-help sphere after years of programming routers and working with innovative technologies being created for next-generation data centers. I had loved my work in the technology field, but my Soul—born into this body under the astrological sign of Aquarius—had other plans.

Corporate work is wonderful because you can focus on your role, project, or area of specialty. As an entrepreneur, however, you are responsible for every role in your company, from sales to marketing to product development to support, and so on. With the leap, I work more hours than I ever did in my corporate role.

With this perspective, my advice is, if you can work off the side of your desk for some time to validate your idea, path, or next steps, please do. Or if you can join committees or boards of directors to align with your passions or your gifts, I hope you pursue these paths first.

Working on your own sounds glamorous, but it can consume many hours of your day without the same benefits as you might receive in a more traditional role.

So be sure to investigate many options for how you can maximize your work and impact.

As you recall, I did not leave my job until I had built up a known revenue stream and undeniable demand, which took six years of working weekends and nights. And even then, it was a big decision to leave my job, and hard to keep everything moving in the right direction.

With this leap, I had nothing to feed my ego while managing my money stories and self-doubt. I am circling around this lesson again because I am sure I am not alone when I share that my self-worth was directly tied to external metrics, which was undeniable when I jumped off the corporate ship, leaving behind whole teams of people who had helped me, lots of paid vacation days, and clear boundaries around my role.

Many women share with me that they, too, define their self-worth by external accomplishments, accolades, and recognition.

How do you determine your self-worth?

_____

_____

When has your self-worth been tested?

_____

_____

What three things or areas boost your sense of self-worth?

_____

_____

If you have lost a job, been demoted, or have gone out on your own, I am sure you have experienced some challenging emotions and maybe even questioned your worth. Work is not the only place where we fill our self-worth bucket.

What close relationships make you question your worth?

_____

_____

How are you being tested to see how much you value yourself, your nudges, and your whispers?

_____

_____

How will you ensure that the energy of others does not activate your self-doubt as you align with your next steps?

_____

_____

Many times it is a reminder for me, too, that no title, salary, or award can top what we do with our bodies to nurture the next generation of human beings. With this important nugget, I often remind women, on calls and from the stage, that our bodies deliver new life to this planet. Some women respond with a knowing smile, while other women disregard this statement.

I feel that it is necessary for all of us to remind each other that women are amazing just as we are. We keep this planet going. Without us, there would be no more life. This is not to discount men's part in the equation, but mothers are often known to nurture their children well beyond childhood. I once heard that if women were in charge, there would be no wars because women are not willing to send their children into battles. I wonder if this would be true.

What I have experienced, with all these external metrics we layer on ourselves and that we adopt from our relationships, is that it is difficult to avoid internal judgment. This inner critic stems from our ego, which drives how we feel about ourselves. And the ego blossoms directly from the stories we have held within ourselves for decades. We have these stories ready and available whenever we are just thinking about exploring something new or interested in changing directions.

These stories can gain even more weight when we layer on the expectations or energies of others. My mom had enough self-doubt on her own, but when she picked my dad to marry, she continued her lesson from her childhood. My dad took the place of her parents, whose actions made her overshadow her own light, further infusing self-doubt into her dreams and decisions. This external energy from the people around her further weighed her down, only adding to her own stories and the related negative energy.

Who weighs you and your dreams down?

_____

_____

What energies from others can you do without?

_____

_____

How will you cultivate the inner strength to rise above your stories and the energies of others?

_____

_____

Why is it worth it to start this week?

_____

_____

These topics are not often openly discussed, as they leave us feeling inadequate, vulnerable, or even alone. Yet these are the *shadow energies* that are lurking in our proverbial closets that we need to shine a light on to usher the darkness out. These often are the energies that fuel our stories and keep us in holding patterns for years.

Yes, I would like to share that I felt confident about getting married, starting my third business after the first two failed, and believing I felt enough self-assurance when I was being tested in my marriage. But no, this was not the case. I felt lonely, unlovable, and scared when it came to saying I had failed. Again. Some nights I cried myself to sleep, and some days I dragged myself to my desk. I worked harder than I thought I could to be a present mother and partner.

The journey is just that: A journey. There are great days and sad days, but the days you make time to work through your self-worth stories are the days that will impact your choices for years to come.

It is okay to say, "I do not like myself" or "I feel worthless" or "I am not enough." I have said these words many times over many years. However, what I can share now is that at least you know where you are starting. As long as you have a desire to make a shift, know that this is the point where you are seeking a new way of living and loving yourself. They are conversations you have with yourself when you know it is time for a shift and you do not want that dark energy taking up any more of your internal space.

Recognizing our internal conversations is a great place to start. Our journeys toward healing start with our relationships with ourselves. Our self-doubts and negative self-talk, fueled by our egos, can derail some good ideas and instrumental work.

But it doesn't have to be that way. We do not have to live a life where our self-worth is aligned with external metrics or negative external voices. We can fuel it, instead, with the sounds of the trees, the voices of centered Souls, and the love we have for the life we created based on choices that are anchored in work that inspires us.

Key Finding #54
You choose what defines your self-worth.

CHAPTER 38

THE FEARS FUELING YOUR SELF-DOUBT

Self-doubt is not an easy thing to admit, especially as we are often taught that a can-do attitude that sidesteps doubts will open doors, land jobs, and get us noticed. Yet self-doubt is a common theme in most women's groups I visit. It often is not discussed head-on, yet many of us can say that, at some point in our lives, we have sat in on talks about imposter syndrome or overcoming our fears.

As I pulled back the layers of self-doubt in my own career and life, I found that most of it was fueled by fears—fear of not being good enough, smart enough, prepared enough, and so on. These fear-based thoughts often stem from the stories we created over the course of our lives.

If I were to ask you, "What are your fears?" some of you would easily be able to admit some of the more common ones—fear of heights, fear of spiders, and fear of snakes. Yet most of us would NOT share the fears that drive so many of our feelings, decisions, and actions. Here is a list of these fears that I have collected over the years from women's events and conversations. These are powerful and deeply impact many life decisions:

- The fear of looking foolish
- The fear of not belonging
- The fear of not being smart enough
- The fear of being seen as not worthy

- The fear of not being loved
- The fear of not being accepted
- The fear of being seen as nothing or irrelevant
- The fear of embarrassment
- The fear of family or friends calling me out
- The fear of feeling stupid
- The fear of being left out
- The fear of not "getting there" (I am still not sure where "there" is, but my ego continues to remind me I have to keep going, as I have a long way to go.)

What fears have been holding you back?

_____

_____

Where do you think these fears stemmed from in your life?

_____

_____

What other fears have a hold on you?

_____

_____

For many of us, fear seems to be the underpinning of what we do or do not do, as we continue to doubt ourselves, what is possible, and what could be. Because of this, many choose to wait until it seems like something has shifted before we further investigate what is possible or even take that step toward our desired goals.

While some of our fears are healthy and keep us aware and out of harm's way, other fears are likely holding us back from stepping into more of our light, our preferred impact, and even our life's work.

We can also flip our fears around to see how they drive us. With a further evaluation of my own fears, I also see that fear can drive us to avoid uncomfortable stories and situations.

- Fear of not having a job
- Fear of being fired
- Fear of not paying the bills
- Fear of being in substantial debt
- Fear of not getting in
- Fear of not being recognized
- Fear of not being seen as a team player
- Fear of not being an equal
- Fear of losing it all
- Fear of being rejected

What are some of your professional fears?

_____

_____

How does fear drive you?

_____

_____

Which of your fears need to be re-evaluated, as they are driving your energy into the ground?

_____

_____

Fear is a tricky emotion. In most circumstances, it camouflages our options and possibilities. Some may use their fears as a tool to push through their doubts to avoid uncomfortable situations, yet many swim in their fears, which prevents them from stepping into their gifts.

I have been known to do both, but now that I am more aware of my fears, I am on the lookout for when those fears are impeding the work I want to do.

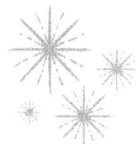

Key Finding #55

Be honest with yourself about the fears that drive and hinder your actions.

CHAPTER 39

RECOGNIZING THE SOURCE OF YOUR ENERGY

It came as no surprise, when I reflected on the times I anticipated a new role, project, or career shift, that I inevitably experienced self-doubt. This ranged from my finances, to my title, to my competency, to my career choices. These thoughts undeniably stemmed from my fears, embedded in my ego, of not being good enough, smart enough, or capable enough.

Of course, I had experiences that proved my fear-based thoughts were incorrect, but even when my inner knowing assured me that I should leap, my ego continued to swoop in. It filled me up with a constant stream of thoughts trying to convince me that I was not ready, and frankly, not capable.

As I think about my thoughts, I have learned to group them in these two boxes:

EGO ENERGY:
FEAR
WORRY
AVOIDANCE

SOUL ENERGY:
ABUNDANCE
LOVE
GRATITUDE

My definitions:

- **Ego Energy**: the energy that comes with our human bodies to protect us.
- **Soul Energy:** the energy that is immersed into our human bodies when we are born that has knowledge, light, and alignment for our work here on Earth.

Our Ego Energy and Soul Energy are constant. One of them leads most days, defining our actions and ultimately our life paths. For many of us, fear takes the lead and is fueled by Ego Energy.

How do you know if fear is winning? You may find yourself thinking or saying the following words:

- I wish…
- When?
- Someday…
- If it works out…
- Not now.
- Not yet.
- I am afraid.
- I can't.
- What will others say?
- I am not ready.
- If only…

What words have you in a holding pattern?

_____

_____

As a child, I remember hearing my family members saying:

- "If we get the bonus check."
- "When we win the lottery."

- "If only we had more extra money."
- "Maybe next time."

What phrases do you remember repeated in your home when you were growing up?

_____

_____

If we look closely, many of us can see trends in the words used throughout our lives, especially when we are thinking about exploring new avenues, making a leap, or changing directions. Can you see how your internal narratives could be driving your decisions and maybe even your path in life?

One way that helped me understand how my ego was impacting my decisions was to monitor my thoughts. Now this may seem like an easy task, but many of us are busy making plans for the future or reflecting on the past. This makes it more difficult to be in the present moment, which is exactly what is needed to track your thoughts.

My most effective technique for making sure I am in the current moment, which is not always easy, is to tap my toes, snap my fingers, or stretch my back. This helps me recognize my thoughts and be aware when my ego is taking center stage and flooding me with negative self-talk.

Once I am present and recognize my internal chatter—the voices or stories in my head that never quit—I take a deep breath and fill my lungs fill up with air. This helps me bring the focus from my head down into my heart area, giving me a break from the constant chatter.

I want to give a big shout-out to Jon Kabat-Zinn for his mindfulness research, training, and teachings. He was a student of Zen Buddhist teachers and now helps people cope with stress, anxiety, and illness with his mindfulness practices. Here is an exercise you can use to bring a keen awareness to your real-time mind chatter.

Thoughts	Anchored in Fear	Anchored in Love	Likely Source	Adjustment or To-Do
I cannot afford that.	X		Lack of money – Childhood	Set aside a small budget to start.
Who do I think I am?	X		Fear of not being enough	Why not *me*?
My family is going to think I am crazy.	X		Family not supporting others' ideas	My family may not support me, but I have a great network of people who do.
I am excited to see what I can do with this idea!		X		Find other people working on similar ideas.
I do not think I am ready!	X		A teacher who might have said, "Always be prepared before you start."	If I am 60% ready, I should go for it, as it can help build my self-efficacy.
Let me see what I can do.		X	I have learned to be curious and try my hand at things.	No expectations. Let me just see what I can do.
I will give myself 30 days		X	Friend – "Set a time limit."	Give it my all for a set time and see what transpires.

Recreate the example table that I have filled in with your own thoughts. Once you get six to twelve reoccurring thoughts listed, take a look at your mind-based chatter, perceived barriers, and potential patterns that show up within your internal stories. It is not uncommon to recognize that many of your thoughts and decisions come from your stories.

Some of us are working with the energy of the ego, and some of us are empowered by the energy of our Souls. Some of us are blocking the abundance and alignment our Souls' energy has to offer. I had to do some work to overcome the mindset of waiting, doubting, and deflecting. I recently listened to a great podcast, *Awaken The Healing–Reclaim Your Life*, Episodes 212, "The 7 Levels of Power," and 221, "Lessons Unlearned." with host Trenayce Talbert.

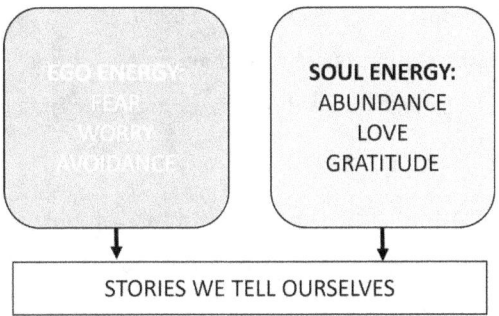

As I stated in previous chapters, our egos are not all bad; they do help us when we find ourselves in intense or trying situations. One big step forward is becoming more aware of the role of the ego in our lives and how it may be hindering our expansion. We need our ego for some protection, but do we have to be safe in our current choices? Is now the time to be safe, or is now the time to explore?

My fears that stemmed from my ego took years to understand. And they still pop up every day. When I recognize I am working from a place of fear rather than a place of abundance, I ask myself:

- Is there a reason to be fearful now?
- Do I really need more_____ to proceed?
- Should I be worried or have anxiety about this situation?
- What can I focus on that can shift my mindset from fear to abundance or appreciation?

I am laughing as I write this because my fears appear more than I would like to admit, even years after practicing to shift the source of my energy from my ego to my Soul. Getting a handle on our fears is not a quick exercise.

1. First, you have to recognize your fears, which comes through noticing your thoughts and internal talk track.
2. Then, you have to intercept them, which may sound easy but often requires you to shift into the present moment, which can be challenging to remember to do.

My mindfulness practice allows me to recognize how fear shows up in my thoughts and how those thoughts might influence my actions. I have learned that I have to actively intercept fear-based thoughts before they impact my decisions and then actions—or lack of action.

If present within myself, I become keenly aware of when my ego kicks in, my fears heighten my insecurities, and then I create a story I tell myself. These stories can take on the narrative of:

- "I am not good enough."
- "I am not smart enough."
- "I should not be doing this now."
- "I am ill prepared."
- "I feel silly."
- "I am not the right person for this."
- "I wish I had their _____."
- "If only I was _____."

Can you relate? The feelings created by any one of these fears could quickly convince me to stay put, not raise my hand, share my opinion, or make my move. The feelings that arise from these stories encourage me to stay in my safe place so no one sees me in a vulnerable state.

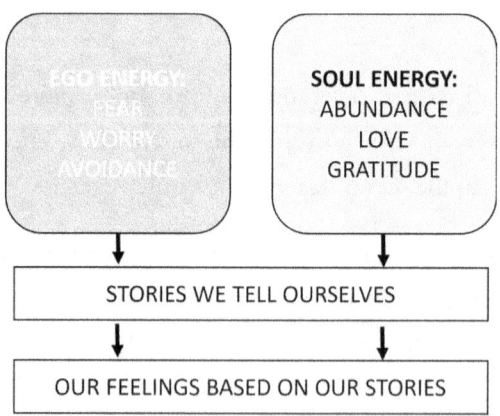

I mentioned *shadow work* in a previous chapter as the work one does to excavate the dark energy and move it out to make more room for light. If the Universe wants you to do some excavation, you might even experience a *dark night of the Soul,* which is similar to a Tower card in the tarot card deck. It often represents difficult or painful situations or times in your life when you are being tested and pushed to move along in your journey. Some Souls get on the other side of these experiences relatively quickly, and some sit in the energy for extended periods of time.

Creating space to go inward and work through the energies that are holding you back can be done with available tools or support, and the process can be very effective. You can now see how your decisions are impacted by these energies.

This internal work is not always easy, I know. It took a lot of mindfulness training for me to learn how to be in the present moment. I had to learn to capture my mind chatter that consisted of reoccurring thoughts as events happened, as decisions needed to be made, and as ideas appeared. Those thoughts are quick and well known to the brain, so if you are not completely present and checking in with yourself, you will likely miss them. Yes, your decisions and actions are often based on quick thoughts, and the source is often your Ego Energy, unless you work to reroute it to your Soul Energy, which encompasses abundance and love.

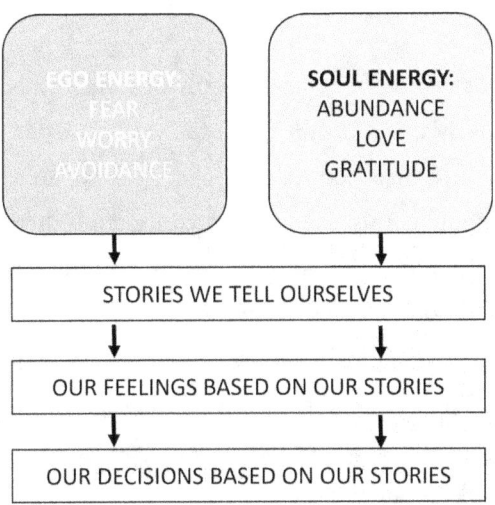

To review this instrumental key finding, our Soul Energy is the immersed energy in our human bodies that works with light, alignment, and love. Unfortunately, this is rarely what initially emerges, as we are conditioned to work from our Ego Energy, which circulates around regulation, judgment, conditioning, repression, denial, and other fear-based energies. I believe one of our biggest lessons in life is to shift our decisions from Ego Energy to Soul Energy.

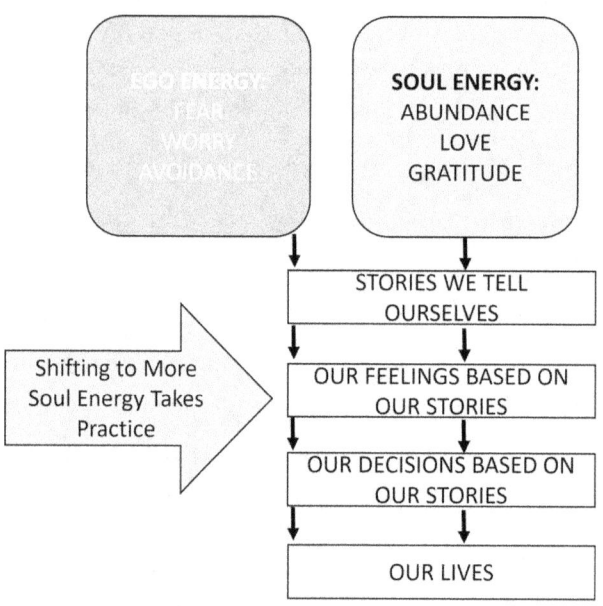

Again, this is not easy at first, but honestly, it formed the basis of my shift in life and work and likely could do the same for you. So try it out, and remember to go easy on yourself. A great tool that helped kickstart my ability to slow down and recognize my thoughts was one of my favorite books by Brené Brown, *Rising Strong: How the Ability to Reset Transforms the Way We Live, Love, Parent, and Lead.* Brené shares specific actions to create separation from your ego by digging into your thoughts and weeding through the emotions. Her work helps you come out on the other side with more self-awareness and more insight into how your thoughts, actions, and outcomes are intertwined and driving your subsequent actions. I highly recommend this book because the practices helped me create a productive and positive space to realign the source of my energy.

Through my work and seeking, I came to believe that we all can benefit from more Soul Energy that focuses on abundance, gratitude, love, and light. With this, monitoring your thoughts and their source is a big step in moving into more self-alignment, joy, and love.

Key Finding #56

The energy you align with, Ego Energy or Soul Energy, will impact your decisions and life's work.

CHAPTER 40

MY CONFIDENCE WALKED OUT THE BACK DOOR

One Spring Saturday morning, I was invited to speak at a women's event on the East Coast. My family joined me, as one of my lifelong friends and soul sisters lived in the area and invited all of us to stay. Our families enjoyed a wonderful dinner Friday night followed by an early bedtime. I remember lying in the bed reviewing my presentation flow and mentally preparing for my talk the next day.

On the morning of the event, I was up early reviewing my slides and timing my delivery. I arrived an hour before the event started, leaving my loved ones at the hotel to discuss their plans for visiting the National Zoo.

I felt nervous, as I do with all my events. Little did I know, I was about to learn a memorable and important lesson on how my ego can sideline my confidence in minutes. I think it is important to note that I describe *self-esteem* as how you feel about something, while your actions, which are based on how you feel, reveal your level of *confidence*.

As the women arrived on that brisk morning wearing colored scarfs and light jackets, I felt confident with the content I planned to share. I had been speaking for a few years on the key points from my book, *The Working Woman's GPS: When the Plan to Have It All Has Led You Astray*, which resonated with women looking for more balance and self-acceptance.

I made my way around the room, saying hello and meeting many of the women as they filled their coffees, networked, and caught up with familiar faces. With a room full of laughter, they were eager to get started.

Instructed by the sounds of bells, we all moved back to our areas and took our seats. I was strategically sitting at the front table off to the right of the stage. The host kicked off the event, which was followed by a wonderful opening speaker who moved all of us during her time on stage. She shared stories of her childhood and the emotional hurdles of the passing of her mother. With few dry eyes in the room, I could feel a wave of emotion take over my thoughts. Within minutes, I found myself questioning both my presentation and my speaking abilities. *How can I follow that? What can I say now that has any importance?*

On the fly, I started reworking my presentation without having any theme or plan. As the audience's applause faded, the MC started to introduce me. I could feel my nerves and sense my self-doubt grow by each passing second. I was already sweating, and my internal voices were loud and unsupportive. My ego stood front and center, leading me with fear and uncertainty.

As I stood up to take the stage, I could feel my confidence walk out the back door. As I spoke, I noticed some odd responses from the audience and definite gaps in my thoughts and delivery. I am being very kind to myself when I say, "My presentation was a flop." I wanted nothing more than to evaporate from that room.

Even as I was sitting back down in my seat, I continued to ask myself, *Why did I agree to this?* Followed by, *I was horrible!* And then, *I am not cut out to be a speaker.*

The women were kind, at least to my face, but I beat myself up that day and for weeks to follow. To this day, I still remember how quickly I sidestepped myself, believing I had nothing worthy of sharing at that moment. I had allowed myself to move off my inner compass as I tried, on the fly, to imitate someone else. The embarrassment was real, and I can still remember how it felt as I approached the stage.

Key Finding #57

Trusting your gifts in times of doubt takes courage.

I have the tendency to mirror others when I am really doubting myself and my value. In fact, I remember one of my spiritual teachers, Rebecca Campbell, talking about the challenge we create for ourselves when we put others on pedestals: "They must come down for you to move up."

Yes, I elevated the speaker before me to a level that I could not reach. In doing so, I let go of my value and abandoned my confidence in my God-given gifts. In that decision, I took an opportunity away from myself and from the women in the room who may have needed my intended message, my offering, and my frequency.

Can you think of a time when you gave away your value or did not trust your gifts?

_____

_____

What was the event or situation that made you question yourself or your offering?

_____

_____

What would you tell yourself now about that situation?

_____

_____

Many practitioners and spiritual guides remind me:

"Learn the lessons you are in right now."

"You are where you are right now for a reason."

What lesson have you been asked to learn from that situation or experience?

_____

_____

How has this lesson appeared in your life at other times?

_____

_____

Time and perspective helped me clarify this and many other lessons, as it is not always easy, especially when I stop to ask, "Why am in this place right now?" and "What do I need to learn from this situation?"

On that brisk Saturday morning, I learned a lesson that I revisit often: No matter how good the speaker, message, or admiration of the audience, *I can choose to step into what God or the Universe has given me to be or to do, or I can step away from it within that moment.*

Trying to show up like the speaker before me or acting like an author I admire might be kind or flattering, but it is not authentic. Putting others on a pedestal is a form of admiration, but it is not healthy for your Soul. We are all here with different gifts, knowings, and insights. If you want to make your mark on this world, you must work to show up and share your authentic offerings as God or the Universe has intended.

Yes, it is likely you will have times, situations, and opportunities in which you think you need to be a certain way to be hired, accepted, or included. You may even go forward with that belief. However, somewhere along the line, the Universe will auto correct by creating a situation that forces you to examine your choices and mindset.

I had liked the speaker before me so much that I thought I should deliver my presentation the same way. Well, I tried to be like her, and surprise, I failed. Had I been more aware of these desires and thoughts as I approached that stage, I would have been able to revert my focus and energy toward delivering from my heart and my gifts.

Instead, I had allowed my mind to take over, and then my ego got the best of me. My ego pushed me into thinking that the only way I would do a good job in that moment was to resemble the awesome speaker ahead of me. This outward focus misled me, and I went down the path of chasing, copying, and imitating.

So, let me save you the embarrassment of mirroring my experience. In fact, I encourage you to lean away from creating the same type of offering, reaction, or response as another person altogether.

These are the words I now use to reassure myself:

I give myself permission to be me.

What I have to share is unique.

I was hand-selected to harness the gifts granted to me.

I am honored to share my gifts with the world.

Key Finding #58
The world needs exactly what you came to share.

CHAPTER 41

MINDFULNESS AND MEDITATION INTERCEPT SELF-DOUBT

How long can we allow self-doubt to influence our decisions? And, at what point does it compromise our life's work?

I am sure you can recall people in your life who shared goals or dreams and then followed their statements with why it was not going to work or stories that supported their self-doubts.

How do we get to a point where we stop ourselves from starting?

From what I have experienced, firsthand and with other professionals, these self-doubts stem from fears that lead to stories about who we are and what is possible. These can stem from one event or encounter, or we could have collected them from others' experiences.

It can be difficult to adjust stories we have adopted along the way, as our egos use them as tools and tee them up on demand. This is what I refer to as *mind chatter* or internal chatter—the specific examples that play out in our heads are often filled with doubt, discomfort, or fear.

The tricky piece is there usually is a sliver of hope embedded somewhere in the story. It is a reassurance we give ourselves that when we get to a certain level or save a specific amount of money or obtain a certain physical state, then we can move forward. But not now. Now we have to stay here, as it is the safest choice.

It is a wicked little trick because it seems that our egos use fear to keep us in holding patterns with some form of hope. Yet if we pay attention, we will find that our hope line moves.

The decisions we make or actions we take are based on the information provided by our egos, and they happen in a split second.

During what events or situations do you notice stories and mind chatter appear?

_____

_____

The great news is that regardless of our mind chatter, we get to decide how we respond to those stories. Even though I have yet to find a way to turn off my mind chatter, and since these thoughts often pepper my aspirations with fears, it is important to counter the noise by creating new practices based in love, gratitude, and curiosity.

Breaking away from this fear, which infuses us with self-doubt, is possible and necessary, even if it's only for small amounts of time and especially when we want to embark on new endeavors or experiences. The words "new," "start," or "try" are just a few of the words that often kickstart our egoic mind chatter.

What are the common triggers for you?

_____

_____

Can you write down the themes or words and phrases that you tell yourself when your ego starts chattering?

_____

_____

If you are not sure exactly what your stories are, you are not alone. Many of us, including me, have spent decades unaware of our mind chatter and how it impacts our self-worth and decisions.

Even more of us have not yet been awakened to the impact these stories have on our lives or even where these stories began. The good news is you are here. With this, you are closer than you think to getting a handle on your internal voice that is working so hard to guide you away from any discomfort or troubles.

If you have a goal or desire or even a thought about moving on from where you are now, the inevitable self-doubt kickstarts the mind chatter that fills you with stories and feelings that are working minute by minute to impact your decisions. Therefore, it is important that you make time to understand your stories and your triggers. With this insight, you can create strategies for identifying and understanding your internal responses and supporting stories, which may be holding you back from your life's work.

As I mentioned, a tool such as mindfulness can help you recognize your stories and mind chatter, which is often necessary before you can embark on raising your frequency and aligning with your life's work. I will admit, mindfulness is not what I thought it was. I tried to learn mindfulness multiple times before I actually grasped the concept. I could not quiet or sidestep my thoughts long enough to truly learn how to be fully aware of the present moment.

For me, learning how to be mindful took practice and patience. With little self-guided progress, I registered for an eight-week mindfulness class with a local instructor, Suzanne Cushwa Rusnak, in 2016. With a notebook in hand, I was initially not an ideal student, but with a great teacher and format designed by Jon Kabat-Zinn (creator of the Stress Reduction Clinic and the Center for Mindfulness in Medicine, Health Care, and Society at the University of Massachusetts Medical School), I eventually gained traction.

An easy way to start is to check out the mindfulness resource, 10 Lessons I Gained from My Mindfulness Practice, I created for you at https://www.jjdigeronimo.com/MindfulnessforWomen. In this free video series, which is less than an hour in length, you will find answers to the following questions:

- Why Is It Difficult to Be Mindful?
- How Can Busy Women Benefit from Mindfulness Training?
- Your Mindfulness Practice: Is There a Connection with Age?
- How Does Meditation Assist with a Mindfulness Practice?

At this point, there should be no surprise that your level of stress, doubt, worry, or anxiety starts with your thoughts. To gain awareness of your thoughts, you must be able to assess your current internal talk track, which for many, takes mindfulness.

Mindfulness paired with meditation has been a game changer for me. It was not until I understood their synergistic relationship that I fully benefited from either. Mindfulness is an active state of being aware of all that is going on in any single moment. Meditation, on the other hand, is a practice that empowers one to be aware of all that is happening in the current moment without attaching to any one thought, idea, or experience.

I had to learn mindfulness before I could become aware of the internal stories that I had playing on repeat and how they were impacting my daily activities and decisions. It was only then that I could meditate. This practice has slowed me down and enabled me to be present.

Being truly present has allowed me to recognize my thoughts and follow them back to stories and then eventually to the events that created them. Then it was possible to work around the stories, which were often inhibitors of action, and instead align with a more purposeful impact.

Mindfulness has:

- Given me space to recognize my self-talk.
- Decoupled me from the badge of "I am so busy."
- Created insight into my inner knowing.

Ask yourself:

- How aware are you of your mind chatter?
- Do you often tell yourself "Not now" before you get started?
- Do you struggle with negative self-talk?

What I have learned, as I expand my mindfulness and meditation practices, is that we are each presented with a series of situations that will test and stretch us to determine if we are spiritually ready for the next lesson or experience.

Lessons that have helped me raise my frequency:

- **Let it go.** Many of us grind too long on the past or worry about the future.
- **Get present.** Our minds often hijack our current moments if we allow them to.
- **Make the time.** It takes meaningful action to understand and manage your thoughts.

Our reality is a mirror image of what is happening within us. If you want to enhance your experiences and alignment in life and work, you must start from the inside and work your way out. Your internal baseline will directly impact how you participate, assess, lead, and contribute at work, at home, and in life.

I personally have to be present to recognize when mind chatter or ego-driven stories begin. Then, I say to myself, out loud: "I got this," or "Step aside, self-doubt." I must interrupt the freight train of unsupportive thoughts that run through my head, impact my confidence, and disrupt my momentum.

What unsupportive stories are on replay for you?

_____

_____

Can you pinpoint how a few of your stories originated?

_____

_____

What have they prevented you from doing, from being, or from moving toward?

_____

_____

Now I will say again that your ego is trying to protect you. With this, you have to determine what to hold on to and what to let go of in that moment. You can only do this if you are living in the moment, and that takes practice. For me, most of my days were spent in my head, planning for events in the future or reflecting on the past. I was fixing, rehashing, rehearsing, planning, changing, and reflecting. All of these mind activities were taking me away from being right here, right now. I had to develop and strengthen a mindfulness practice that supported my meditation practice.

Taking time to slow down and assess what is impacting your decisions is a critical piece for empowering yourself to go and to be in this lifetime. To do this, you must check in on your level of self-doubt related to something new. Do you hold back because it is not the right time, or you do not have the money, or you are not ready?

Being mindful of your internal chatter and then managing it fiercely so it does not derail, discourage, or hold you back is necessary for you to reach your desired goals. These internal stories and thoughts, if not intercepted, will happily impact your decisions, self-worth, and future actions.

Remember, you have the power to overcome those negative thoughts that could impact you while you are trying to reach your goals. With this perspective, you can investigate a path that makes sense for you.

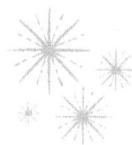

Key Finding #59

Unmanaged mind chatter fuels our self-doubt, hijacking new experiences, work, and impact.

CHAPTER 42

THE PRESENT OF MINDFULNESS

If you know there is more for you to accomplish, learn, discover, and impact during this journey on Earth but are not sure where to start or how to activate your ideas, you are not alone. Knowing is the first step in honoring yourself for wanting to step out in a new way.

Many women come to me with questions, such as: "Where do I start? How do I find more joy? Can I too create more room for light? Who should I talk to about my ideas?"

Every journey is different. My solo trip to Sedona in 2013 kicked off a rebirth of seeking new levels of insight and reassurance. Trusted friends and family members were often my sounding boards, yet since then, I also turn to many Energy Practitioners and Lightworkers who share their positive energy and knowing to help me illuminate my inner wisdom. Through calls, webinars, in-person meetings, and podcasts, I now work to incorporate all the messages that come my way to guide my journey.

My initial advice to those looking to expand their journeys is to work on being present as often as possible. This is not always easy, yet an active mindfulness practice will be instrumental to shift from Ego Energy to Soul Energy. Through this, the Universe provides opportunities to align with new activities and people. Continuously listen, watch, and ask.

I know I would not have recognized many of my messages if I was multi-tasking or allowing my ego to hijack my current moments. I have learned that I must slow down, both physically and mentally, which takes practice.

Key Finding #60

Being present is one of the greatest gifts I have given myself.

Quick Exercise: Get Present in Minutes

Find fifteen minutes in your schedule, a quiet space, and a comfortable seat. Bring a notebook or piece of paper with you. Set your timer for fifteen minutes. When you start the time, observe everything around your selected area and write down everything you experience.

Now fifteen minutes is a long time to be observing, so do not be surprised if you initially run out of things to write down. Remember, you can use all five senses as you take in your surroundings. This is a judgment-free space, so observe, log, and move on. If you find yourself adding comments to your observations, such as "I need to water that plant" or "That wall needs a new coat of paint," recognize that you have drifted into creating future tasks. Instead, focus on identifying and logging without letting your mind have an opinion or additional thoughts about the item listed. Feel free to revisit things you observe multiple times, recognizing other aspects or new interpretations. For example, if you logged a TV, consider capturing any reflection on the screen, or shift your awareness to what you hear. What sounds you are hearing around your space? Consider grouping some of your views. If you have a plant, how many leaves are pointing North?

After a fifteen-minute session, consider these questions:

How hard was it to stay focused and present?

_____

_____

When your mind wandered, how did you bring it back to the present moment?

_____

_____

What did you expect from this exercise, and how did it differ from your expectations?

_____

_____

What was the hardest part?

_____

_____

What did you enjoy, or what surprised you?

_____

_____

What other thoughts tried to occupy your mind?

_____

_____

Each time you practice being in the current moment, you will work to remind your ego that there is more to you than the mind chatter and stories it serves up on a regular basis. Being present takes time and practice, especially with an active mind that wants to be productive.

A mindfulness practice can help you recognize the non-stop chatter that many of us experience, distracting us from the present moment. One way to keep working on being in the present moment is to set your next observation time every time you end.

As you work through the future chapters, it is important that you prioritize this inside work to shift from Ego Energy to Soul Energy. So many times we have wanted to get to the other side or get things behind us, only to get there and realize we are not in alignment, or we did not ground the idea, or we did not take the path desired in fear of it not working out.

Fear holds us back in so many ways. Having tools can help you decide which fears are essential from a safety perspective and which are limiting beliefs holding you back from your next step and maybe part of your life's work.

What can you do today to create more mindfulness practices throughout your week?

_____

_____

I must admit that I needed a good push to get a mindfulness practice underway in my life. Now, looking back, I realize it was perfectly positioned by an unlikely source, which I now see as a guide—Dr. Jill, my short-term therapist.

Dr. Jill asked, "JJ, why are you here?"

"I am seeking inner peace." I felt foolish saying those words.

"Can you elaborate?" she asked.

"I want more than laughter and good times. I want to feel whole, loved, and complete. I am seeking inner peace and more joy!"

"Why don't you have joy?" she asked.

"I don't know, as I have so many things to be joyful for but I feel disconnected."

As expected, she had more questions, and my answers all seemed to circulate around, "I need to find out how to love myself for what I am and not for what I do, create, or deliver."

I added that I also wanted to "drop the self-doubt, negative talk, and demands I put on myself to get there."

She tilted her head, wrote a few more notes, and then asked, "Where is 'there'?"

My voice cracked. "I don't know." I am sure she could feel the sadness in my voice, as I felt embarrassed by my answer.

I found myself saying, "When I get there, I can _____!" *Where is there, and why is here not there? Ugh!*

I knew consciously that joy was all around me, but I did not have the right lens or the tools to be in the present moment so I could experience it. Instead, I was mentally consumed with *What's next? What's due? What needs to be done?* A mindset that had me rushing from one thing to the next so I could be more productive, dependable, and effective. Only to find myself tired, depleted and, at times, alone.

Can you relate?

Where do you experience joy?

_____

_____

What gets in the way of your joy?

_____

_____

What is holding you back from experiencing more joyful moments?

_____

_____

Are you so busy doing, working, and strategizing for what is ahead that you miss opportunities to have fun, create joy, and enjoy the fruits of your labor? I knew I was missing the joy train.

Unfortunately, I did not think I had good examples of people ahead of me telling me to slow down, enjoy, or be present. That is not fair, because I may have had men and women sharing their wisdom, but I was too focused on and too driven by chasing the oasis of success, power, financial freedom, and so on.

And then Dr. Jill was strategically placed in my life. Without hesitation, she firmly recommended an eight-week mindfulness class, in-person, that met every Sunday from 1:00 p.m. to 3:00 p.m.

My first thought was, *Not an ideal time with kids in sports and family gatherings; this is not possible.* I admit, I thought about this class every time she recommended it. But on our third visit, she made it mandatory if I wanted to see her again.

At first, I was shocked that she would be so bold and annoyed that she would push me to do something I was not ready to commit to at that moment. I now see that her request was a life test to see how much I wanted fulfillment, joy, and even alignment on the inside.

I am the first to say that I can be stubborn, but I generally come around in time. It took me about a month to sign up, but it has been one of the best-guided nudges I have received in my life. Thank you, Dr. Jill, for being so determined to get me in that seat.

Years later, mindfulness is one of the key tools I recommend to others. It shines a bright light on our self-doubts and the fears that fuel them, as we are front and center, seeing it all play out in our minds. Even more than seeing what is happening on the inside, we have a front-row view of what and who crosses our paths.

Being present gives us the choice on what energy and mind chatter we are going to listen to and act upon. Shifting from Ego Energy to Soul Energy with mindfulness empowers all aspects of our lives, including passion projects, inspiring interactions, and future initiatives. I would have to guess that buried inside much of these meaningful decisions, connections, and work, there are glimpses of our life's work, too.

Key Finding #61

Being present is the underpinning of raising your level of awareness, joy, and enlightenment.

CHAPTER 43

TOO BUSY TO CELEBRATE

It was a hot summer day in Ohio. I was enjoying my coffee while on the phone with a dear friend who was expecting the boxes of her first book to arrive that afternoon. I was so excited for her, as I remember the days in July 2011 and September 2016 when the boxes of my new books arrived on my doorstep.

Turning in a clean manuscript to the publisher is so exhilarating, but then months go by before you can hold that book in your hands. Many authors I know anticipate this day, including me, when they decide to write a book, as the steps from idea, to draft, to multiple reviews, to layout, to publication can be tedious.

Amy was no different. She experienced many twists and turns during the publishing process, with hurdles at many key milestones that delayed her printing and shipment dates. Focused on her missed opportunities and overwhelming list of to-dos, she said, "JJ, I think you are more excited for this moment than I am."

That heaviness was all too familiar. I could feel her words hit my heart. With my old "get it done" approach to life that used to sit in my head, I would have felt so far behind too, with a desperate need to catch up for the lost time. I felt as sad for my friend as I did for myself. The nagging voice in our heads that often acts as a joy zapper was making an appearance, and I could feel the familiar disappointment.

Key Finding #62
Infuse love and self-acceptance into a joy-zapping mindset.

Excitement and a sense of accomplishment should have filled that morning. Yet many of us are hurrying to get on to the next thing. Through all this rushing, we often miss the moments of joy available for us to embrace.

This is not uncommon. When I ask, "When is the last time you experienced joy?", many people share big life moments such as a wedding, birth, significant trip, or large purchase. Few respond with ordinary moments, such as something in nature, a glass of wine with a friend, or attending a child's activity.

I, too, used to seek the extraordinary events to fill my joy bucket. The rest of the time, I focused on driving my task toward completion, which blinded me to ordinary yet magical moments. Yes, I too was so good at getting things done or pushing things forward that I lost out on many moments during my ordinary days that were joyful.

With my work and lessons, I did not want Amy to miss out by pushing beyond these ordinary yet joyful moments, as I had done for so many years. It is sometimes hard to slow down, so I continued to highlight for Amy the significance of this delivery as a time to enjoy and embrace. I shared, "This is a day to celebrate" many times during our call. I wanted to quickly teach her how to drop down from her head into her heart. I am able to do this to align with more love and gratitude rather than fear and doubt. While Amy did not talk about fears and doubt, her desire to catch up was a disguised fear of falling behind or not being seen as good enough.

I continued to encourage her to be in the moment. I reminded her that all the things on her to-do list could be done later, or even the next day. I would not let up. "Amy, embrace the arrival of your first book on your doorstep today. This is a moment that you deserve. Give yourself time to appreciate and honor all the work, hours, and commitment it took to make this happen. Take sixty to ninety seconds to jump up and down or feel the sunlight on your face, as you have birthed a new source of information for people. Take a picture of the moment, and if needed, lie down on top of the boxes to express the labor of love needed to make this book a reality."

She laughed. "I will try to be in the moment for thirty seconds." And then she quickly followed up with why she was over it and needed to get things done, as she had a big week ahead.

How often do you push aside moments of joy to make room for what is next on the list?

_____

_____

What moments of joy have you missed out on this week?

_____

_____

Can you take a minute to look around and pick something to be joyful for right now?

_____

_____

Feeling unheard and deflated, I knew my words were floating away into the ether. There was a time not too long ago when many shared their experiences and lessons with me, but I was not really available or ready to hear or absorb them.

You might be glossing through this book or diving in. Wherever you are in your journey will determine what you hold on to and what lessons you absorb.

As you know, it was not an overnight shift for me. I started my mindfulness course three times before fully committing to it. I listened to more than fifty books and committed at least three hours a week to invest in my journey of self-discovery. These choices took time, self-love, and a commitment to me and my journey. I had some stops and starts, repeats and revisits, but I eventually fostered a new level of self-acceptance that is not tied to external metrics, which I had the hardest time uncovering. Now, I have a newfound love for being in the moment, which took more than six years to adopt and embrace.

I look forward to sharing a few more of my key findings to take your seeking to a new level. The insights in future chapters include tools I used to raise my frequency and uncover more of my life's work. I hope you are ready to absorb a little bit more.

Key Finding #63

Only you can shift unrealistic expectations into more meaningful and memorable experiences.

PART V

SHIFTING YOUR FREQUENCY

CHAPTER 44

LASSO YOUR ENERGY

If you find yourself in a position where you are questioning yourself, your offerings, or your talents, don't be alarmed. This is normal. I find that bringing myself back to the current moment is critical and instrumental in ensuring my mind does not take me down a path of no return.

If you are not sure if you are in the moment, then tap your toe, purposefully move your fingers, or slowly feel yourself breathing through your nose. Once you are present, you can often recognize the ego-based doubts running through your head.

What do you do to ground yourself in the moment, especially when you have self-doubts?

_____

_____

Do you experience anxiety, or does your heart race?

_____

_____

Do your doubts take you in another direction or stop your excitement or momentum?

_____

_____

How do you feel about your doubts and your decisions?

_____

_____

Where can you feel your doubts in your body?

_____

_____

A big lesson for me is to be present not only with what is happening around me but also within me—where I am feeling the most unsettled within my body. Sure, my heart might be beating fast, but it is often my head that feels heavy and very busy.

Assessing the energy within your body is essential to understand how you are holding and processing the flow that is likely impacting your thoughts and your next action. This is especially important if you sabotage situations that are opportunities to experience and align with more joy.

In the past, I had been holding on to my stories, which created a flurry of mind chatter, and I had acted upon them as if they were non-negotiable. They had heavily influenced my confidence, decisions, and choices. I had not realized that I had the ability to manage my mind chatter.

With more knowing, I have learned how to drop my internal focus from my head down into my heart—aligning with my heart chakra. Chakras are key points inside or outside our bodies that are focal points of circulating energy. It took me some time to learn how to focus on and then realign energy inside and around my body to create a more peaceful way of living.

Once I tap my toes or snap my fingers to get into the present moment, I can then conduct a quick inventory of what and where the energy is active in my body. When I am anxious or nervous, I can often feel the energy swirling around in my head. I focus on the feeling, as big or small as it might be, and I put an imaginary lasso around it.

The shift of energy from my head to my heart is necessary for me to sidestep the stories, boundaries, and barriers that my ego spoon feeds me any time I am looking to reach, seek, stop, start, or expand.

When I visually lasso that hectic momentum in my head and usher it down into my heart chakra, that internal force is often softer and more accepting of me, myself, and my actions. This shift often creates the space and time I need to go easy on myself and evaluate my choices with love rather than fear.

I sometimes find that the energy can be stubborn and uninterested in my desire to guide it out of my head and down into my heart. To be sure I did not leave any of that chaotic energy up in my head, I often visually take a cruise around my brain to be sure I got it all. And if I find a few pockets of lingering turmoil, I usher it down to my heart, leaving my head some free time to simmer down my anxiety. More often than not, the energy that circulates in my head is fueled by fear, uncertainty, or self-doubt. With this shift, I can often make decisions with more love and light rather than fear and anxiety.

It took me some time to figure out how to harness and lasso this energy down into a place of empathy and love, which, for me, is around my heart. You can practice different ways of moving energy in your body. Some people like to visualize the tops of their heads opening and letting that energy fly out like butterflies, and other people usher the energy down through their bodies and back into the earth through their feet.

Fear often appears quickly for many of us, but there is no reason to let that fear fill you with uncertainty or confusion because you are powerful, wise, and resourceful. You are light and filled with love, but the ego is determined to make you feel otherwise. Trust that each experience, including this book, is crossing your path on purpose. There are lessons all around us to experience, as our journeys are uniquely designed for each of us.

That Saturday morning presentation where my confidence walked out the backdoor brought forward a key lesson for me that I still find beneficial: Each of us has unique gifts to share with the world. Don't doubt yourself, your offerings, and your work. Your light is bright, and you are magical! Never forget that you have been hand-selected to share your gifts, wisdom, and insights your way.

Your gifts are needed now more than ever. Don't spend time questioning yourself. You are ready to share your wisdom right now!

What are three difficult situations you have encountered that you can now see as key lessons for your life?

1. _____

2. _____

3. _____

Remember, you are fiercely equipped to move through life sharing your gifts, but sometimes you have to recalibrate your inner compass and the energy that fuels it. Shifting the energy from your head down to your heart could be the shift you need to accelerate your journey.

Key Finding #64

You have the power to shift your energy at any time.

CHAPTER 45

THE ENERGY YOU RADIATE

In my experience, it is a rarity for a person's energy to shift from negative to positive or vice versa without a purposeful catalyst helping the transition. Often when people are feeling negative or frustrated, each new element that crosses their paths tends to exacerbate their feelings.

Take a minute to think about your energy level or frequency. Are you working to raise your vibration or maintain your flow? Are you weighing people down with your complaining and unsettled energy, or are you lifting others up?

What energy do you often share with others?

_____

_____

What energy do you choose to hold on to, and what energy do you let go of?

_____

_____

What energy do you cultivate within yourself?

_____

_____

I recently experienced a noticeable energy exchange while traveling with my two children from Seattle to Ohio. We had attended a beautiful family wedding on Whidbey Island off the coast of Seattle in Washington State. During the long weekend, in addition to the wedding, we visited a national park, picked wild blackberries, and hiked parks and roadside paths. We had covered hundreds of miles, and I was tired. I was looking forward to the five-hour flight home and planned to watch movies and tackle my emails.

As we boarded the plane and found our seats, my aisle neighbor and I made eye contact and shared pleasantries. It wasn't long before I could feel the anxious energy that consumed her. Most of us have some ability to empathically connect with other people's energy. My abilities as an empath have expanded over the years because I have continued to clean out my stories, let go of internal darkness, and align more with light and love.

Moments after feeling her unsettled energy, I witnessed an odd exchange of energy between her and the flight attendant; she demanded a soda as other passengers were still boarding. We were not in first class, so her asking for a drink in economy-class before departure seemed unusual, but I thought, *Maybe she has low sugar.*

I was excited to be on a flight home with my two kids. I fly often, but not with them. I enjoy traveling with them, as they bring so much humor and awareness to our adventures. I didn't want the energy from my rowmate to impact my experience, so to preserve this joy, I shifted my body toward my kids.

Shortly after the doors were closed, the pilot announced a ninety-minute delay due to weather. The woman in my row shifted her focus from needing a soda right this minute to the fear of not making her connection. I was curious; did she realize that our energy usually attracts similar energy?

Like a radio frequency, her frustration and negativity radiated out of her seat to all of us around her. To shield my own frequency, I pressed my feet to the floor to create a path for all her negativity that came my way to flow right into the ground. Then, I shifted all my positive energy and attention to my left, where my kids were happily getting settled into their areas and picking out their movies. Watching them travel warms my heart. I love how much they enjoy each trip.

As the next ninety minutes unfolded, the energy exchanges happening around me covered the spectrum. My kids contentedly opened their snacks and adjusted their headphones. In front of us was a cute older couple, excited and on their way to visit their great-grandbabies. Kitty corner from me sat a young professional already drifting off to sleep, while the lady across the aisle from me was making her frustrations known.

The different energy exchanges between the flight attendants and these different passengers within arm's length of my seat were noticeable. The flight attendant was so sweet to the older couple, and left the young professional alone to sleep, and then shifted her energy during the interaction with the demanding woman across from me.

Key Finding #65

The energy you radiate alters and impacts the energy you receive.

In my first book, *The Working Woman's GPS*, I wrote a chapter called "Practicing Polluter" for a specific person in my life. Our initial relationship was not by choice; she married a person who often attended the same gatherings as I did. When I initially met her, I felt for her, as her life had taken a series of bad turns. Without getting into too much detail, it appeared that she chose, maybe not consciously, to be the victim. Yes, she had some bad luck and a few bad people in her life, but she also had many opportunities to shift toward more gratitude. Day after day, however, she chose to focus on the negative.

She had many blessings to be counted, including funds at her disposal, her health, and her family. Maybe she was unaware that she had choices, or she was so altered as a child that she could not find a way back to her light, or maybe this was not her time for those lessons. Regardless of why she chose to view life through a negative lens, she made a practice of drowning any available listeners with her doom and gloom, hence the practicing polluter analogy.

I am sure you can think of people in your life who are often frustrated, disappointed, or find problems within their circumstances. Some may be like this all the time, and others get revved up about a specific topic.

Think about the people in your life or your favorites within your phone app or social media pages. Think about who you look forward to talking with and why. Then think about who you dread talking with and why. If you have read any of my other books, you know I love charts. They are easy ways to assess what is happening right now and what is working for you.

Person's Initials	Relationship Duration	Positive Frequency	Negative Frequency	Topics to Avoid	Rate the Impact on Your Life

After listing the person's initials, be sure to add the length of time you have known her or him, because people who are around you for a few years or months are very different from people connected to you for decades. Then decide if their usual energy is positive or negative and, if needed, add some topics that set them off.

A woman I worked with had a significant other who refused to let her change jobs. He was generally positive except when she wanted to do something different, which would go into the "topics to avoid" column. This, of course, had a substantial impact on her life, but her fear of being alone was greater than her desire to shift. After a few years of working together, I learned that her mother had many relationships, and she had no desire to repeat her mother's path, so she stayed inside the barriers created by her need to be in a relationship.

A girlfriend of mine had a mother who was judgmental and often rude. My friend was kind. She would call her mother every Sunday, not because she wanted to but because she would never hear the end of it from her mother and father if she did not make that call.

One afternoon, I was with her during her weekly call and was shocked by her mother's words. My friend shared that she was used to it and had to get it off her weekly list, but I could see the energy shift in my friend.

We had many long talks about this, and she has made great strides with setting boundaries and not allowing her mother to talk to her in specific ways or with certain tones. The point is, you decide what energy you let near and around you, as others' energy can and often will impact your frequency. If your desires and seeking have taken you to new information or even new places, you need to work to protect your frequency.

When it comes to energy, there are no straight lines. Energy bounces, jumps, ricochets, and aligns, so there is no escaping your energy or other people's energy. We must be aware of the people that we allow into our spheres.

- What do we do with the energy they share?
- What energy do we share?
- Do we create good energy together?

Being consciously aware of the energy you share is crucial to your life's equation. And you may quickly say to yourself, *I am positive* or *I share kindness* or *I am nice*, but being aware of your thoughts is one key finding, and another is what you say to yourself and others. Some mask their negativity as "Look what happens to me," "Can you believe how I was treated?" or "Why am I the unlucky one?"

Many of us give ourselves permission to turn negative if we are reacting to an event or situation—a bad driver, an annoying co-worker, disrupted travel plans, or family issues. Just remember that if you allow it, you might find that your frequency drops within minutes. In such situations, recall that life is happening for you and not to you. These situations present you with opportunities to drop down into your heart chakra and then determine what is best for you, your journey, and your life's work.

During this specific flight from Seattle, it was even more apparent to me that we were all heading in the same direction that day. Yes, we had different relationships, experiences, upbringings, and mindsets, but we all came together on that plane. How we each responded to the same experiences, exchanges, and situations varied widely, even though we were all heading in the same direction. Our individual approach to our circumstances can make or break our experiences.

Key Finding #66

Supervise and protect your frequency.

CHAPTER 46

YOUR FUEL STATIONS & GALACTIC CHIPS

What empowers, inspires, and excites you? Yes, it could be a big trip or an influx of funds, but beyond the big-ticket items that people dream of, what makes you feel good?

Knowing the things that create positive, purposeful, and elevated energy for you are your fuel stations. These are sources that create positive energy and can increase your frequency.

Often these activities are associated with your passions that you likely had a glimpse of as a child. They might not be creating a lavender farm, but I bet some of the clues are buried in your childhood. I encourage you to make time to think about some of your clues if it is difficult to know what empowers, inspires, and excites you.

Prioritizing your energy level is essential, as it starts from within, with many external and internal attempts to drive your frequency down. It takes a commitment to tap into your gifts and desired frequency.

An easy way to elevate your energy and even your joy is to focus on gratitude for what already is. From the ten days of gratitude exercise in Chapter 25: Money Carries the Frequency We Give it, we know shifting into gratitude and purpose takes a mindset that is present, aware, and loving.

On the night before my flight with my kids from Seattle to Ohio, my Soul sister and lifelong friend's daughter Aspen, who was eleven years old at the time, shared the story of Galactic Chips with my kids.

Aspen and her family frequently travel far and wide, from South America to New Zealand and beyond. Consequently, they often experience travel delays, reroutes, and cancellations. Aspen shared that Galactic Chips are collected as travel plans go wonky or downright disastrous. These imaginary chips are then exchanged at a later time when things work in their favor, like a standby clears or an upgrade is granted.

Aspen emphasized the importance of staying positive and appreciative rather than disappointed and frustrated. I was so delighted by her story, and watching my kids, who were ten and twelve years old at the time, listen to her specific examples of how her family choose gratitude when things went sideways was even more magical.

It reminded me about a nugget I gathered from Jen Sincero's book *You Are a Badass*. Jen shares a specific approach that I love and have already adopted and share often. When faced with a challenging experience, say to yourself: "This is good because . . . ." I love this approach because if you want to raise your frequency, you must alter the way you view, digest, and respond to situations, events, and mishaps. When put into practice, this lesson is one of the most important elements I have adopted to elevate my energy. I can attest that this simple sentence starter, "This is good because . . . ." can directly impact how I feel, how much joy I experience, and what I attract into my life.

So, take some time to monitor your exchanges, energy level, and outlook within situations you encounter.

Where can you use the words "This is good because . . . ." in your life right now?

_____

_____

What situations invoke your not-so-positive self (practicing polluter tendencies)?

_____

_____

When do you get excited about your experiences or exchanges with others?

_____

_____

When do you attract the wrong energy?

_____

_____

When do you or can you collect Galactic Chips?

_____

_____

What negativity do you more intentionally need to release or avoid?

_____

_____

Are you mindfully aware of the energy you share, or are you operating in cruise control?

_____

_____

Do you know a few more of your fuel stations, or do you need time to explore?

_____

_____

With a focus on creating, sharing, and inspiring yourself and others, your fuel stations can be instrumental to your seeking.

With this, it might be challenging at times to find the support you desire, but knowing your fuel stations is critical to aligning with energy that empowers you.

As with most examples in this book, I am sharing a variety of ways you can raise your frequency, sidestep your self-doubt, and align with your life's work. You are the only one who knows which way is best for you, and it takes quiet time and mindfulness to capture the whispers. Here is a note from Kristina, a woman I met at a tech event in

Texas after my presentation, who generously sent me this note about how she listens to her whispers and aligns with her fuel stations:

Hey JJ,

I hope you've had a great start to your week. Last week, I had my last day in the office. Still employed by WD for a few months, thanks to a severance package, but don't have to work. I moved/drove from Boulder to Austin, and now I am in New Zealand for 3 weeks visiting family/friends/home.

I wanted to make sure I stayed in touch with you and let you know my updates. I'd love to connect with the lady you met in Austin at some point as well. Taking this route (no job) is scary and exciting all at once, and I'm confident I'll land somewhere amazing. I just don't want to be ignorant and assume anything will happen without me being proactive.

Getting to come home (NZ) for a few weeks is my "filling station." Nothing brings me more peace and joy than being here with my family and friends. I figured many job openings will be set for early 2020, so taking this much needed time to fill up and center was the best thing for me.

I hope you're well and I look forward to connecting with you again.

Best regards,

Kristina

Where can you lean into your fuel stations?

_____

_____

I love Kristina's note, as it showcases how she is making the best of her situation. She is living in a way that showcases how every event, condition, or exchange can provide insights and potential lessons. Some of these lessons may come through a series of events, and others through the people around you.

Remember, the people who have supported you to date may or may not be interested in supporting you as you align with your future. This can be especially true if you decide to prioritize more of what is calling you and less of what you have been doing for them.

Energy Practitioners and Lightworkers have been instrumental in my process of seeking. They have helped me decouple my own interdependencies and the unhealthy expectations of others who were trying to distract me from my fuel stations.

If you think you could use some assistance in creating more space and light within your schedule and life, Lightworkers can be great advocates to help you work through your stories and connections with other Souls. More light and love are available for you right now, if you are ready to prioritize your actions and energy exchanges.

Having gratitude, along with an acute awareness of your fuel stations, are beautiful gifts you can tap into at any time. These will empower you to experience the good energy. Collecting, creating, and sharing Galactic Chips elevates your frequency, harnessing the inner strength necessary so you can sidestep your self-doubts and prioritize your work.

Key Finding #67

Be mindful of the energy you create and collect.

CHAPTER 47

YOUR STORIES, YOUR BOUNDARIES, AND YOUR SEASONS

At the end of a large event where I delivered a ninety-minute Align with Your Next Level of Impact workshop, I was approached by a tall, sun-kissed woman in casual attire. She was clearly ready to connect and jumped right into her question.

"What if I am not aspiring to impact anything new right now?"

I smiled as I realized that I did not mention to the group, "Sometimes in your life, you are taking in the view, appreciating your journey, and/or keeping things afloat. Not all of us are in motion at the same time or on the same path. Taking a breath, slowing down, and being in the moment is a gift you can always give yourself."

One of my favorite authors, Rebecca Campbell, states in her blog post "Rising and Falling and Falling and Rising," "We are cyclic beings living in a cyclic world and we are not made to bloom (rise) all year round. And, the greatest rising (blooming) comes after the most significant falls (letting go/releasing). The seasons teach us how to rise each and every year. If we do not honor that process and attempt to stay blooming all year 'round, holding onto our leaves tightly, come Spring, there will be no space for the new to bloom."

I was not able to recite Rebecca's words exactly, but what I was able to remember about the changing of the seasons and the cycles of the flowers seemed to provide some relief to the lovely woman before me. So much so that she continued to share her journey with me. I listened to her every word, as I knew by her effortless stance and vibrant energy that she had done the inside work. Little did I know she was going to share these nuggets of wisdom with me.

Five years ago, she adopted a new way of living. Every month she committed to adding one new action to improve how she felt about herself.

- Month 1: She started going to the gym three days a week.
- Month 2: She invested in her smile and straightened her teeth.
- Month 3: She invested in eye surgery so she could see the beauties of the world.
- Month 4: She started mindfulness and meditation training so she could quiet her mind, appreciate all she had to offer, and work around her self-doubt.

As the months progressed, she became more comfortable in her skin and more decisive in her words and actions. With her increasing self-worth and love, her marriage disintegrated at an equal pace.

Now divorced, she is straddling numerous time-consuming responsibilities, including parenting, driving her children, taking care of elderly parents, delivering at work, leading a global team, and now, dating, which she is happy to add to her list. Just listening to the list, I started to feel tired, but even with all these responsibilities, she glowed, and her tone was upbeat.

She added, "Although I want to advance my career, since I'm already fifty-one, I feel like I already have too many things in motion."

I reassured her that not all things "bloom" at the same time and being selective is just as important as deciding what needs to be the priority or needs to change.

I found it interesting that she mentioned her age and asked why she added that level of detail. She said she feared being too old or not being an obvious choice for others. She continued to explain how her current situation may prevent her from moving into more passion-based work.

I reassured her that she had way too much positive energy to be overlooked and that she could create her new reality whenever she was ready. With this, I delicately mentioned that the world needs all of us.

Although some of you might be counting down to retirement, your retirement years can be more of an energy shift, depending on what you prioritize and decide to impact. I often refer to this as a chapter change in life, a time when many things shift and you get to decide what will be in the next chapter of your life. This definitely does not have to be based on age. It can happen when things in your life shift or people that used to be around move along.

Even with her tremendous energy and momentum, there were still stories she told herself. A few I quickly captured: "I am getting old," "I cannot retire," "How will I support myself?" "I am divorced now. This is going to be hard," and "What will happen to the people who depend on me?" These concerns and fears impacted how she felt about the future, even skewing her vision and making her question her abilities and timeline.

As you think about your journey, timeline, and stories, ask yourself:

What season am I in right now? (Blooming in spring, hibernating in winter, enjoying the fruits of my work in summer, or winding down in the fall.)

What am I doing to invest in myself?

What stories are preventing me from moving toward my whispers or desired projects?

Who would fall out of my sphere of energy if I prioritized me more often?

_____

_____

How do I feel about those things or people moving out of my main energy sphere?

_____

_____

How have I given up on what is important to me in this lifetime?

_____

_____

How can I incorporate one thing a week that excites me?

_____

_____

Our lives are journeys with many steps and lessons along the way. Honoring where you have been and what you have learned is a vital piece of gratitude that is necessary before you can evolve toward new experiences and lessons.

There is no need to second guess where you are or have been. Now is the time to be honest about the fears that continue to creep up. Some popular ones are the fear of inconveniencing others or the fear that "I will not be ready or good enough."

We are not expected to bloom all the time, but we also need to realize that we cannot live in winding down (Fall) or hibernation (Winter) either. Although my mother talked about divorce since I was twelve years old, she never left my father. I think the fear of starting over and doing it all on her own was too overwhelming. I think that would have scared me too if I was her at that time in our society. Fortunately, things on the planet are shifting again for women.

Yet, I still harbor sorrow for my mother, as she retired over fifteen years ago and had big plans, but days turned into nights, and months turned into years. This happens to many of us. We leave this planet only using a fraction of our gifts, even though we intend to explore more of those whispers. Unfortunately, time runs out for some.

It is not easy, as there is always more to do, but what I have learned along my journey is when you let go of striving for more, you can free up space to look at what you already have.

Being grateful for who we are and what we already have empowers us to look for the good, get inspired by what is, and even nourish our gifts. We do not have to have any more degrees, more titles, more days, or anything right now to tap into the difference we want to make. We can start small or big, regardless of our age or experience, as we have everything we need right now to do our life's work. We came equipped with the tools we needed to do what we agreed to do while we are here.

It can be challenging to make the time, so finding peace and passion within your yeses is essential. You can always revisit my free course, *The Power of No*, to help you find or make the time for the activities that excite you. The acts of creating the space and time to visit your fuel stations or share your gifts can often act as catalysts for your future shifts and alignment.

Had I not made the time to visit Dr. Jill and then make a more significant investment in myself by signing up for my mindfulness class on a Sunday afternoon, I am not sure how much of this may have unfolded in the last few years. It is likely the Universe would have circled back around in different ways at different times to move me along. That being said, there is no guarantee that we will be open to the messages and invites, as many of us are swimming in fear, self-doubt, and worry, so it is up to us to create that openness.

Luckily for me at that time, I listened to the whispers and was ready to prioritize myself and my joy. With that series of decisions, the flow of information, support, and people have ushered me along. Books, connections, invites, and messages have moved me through my lessons, aligning me each step of the way into my life's work, which I believe has brought me here with you.

What you decide to focus on, where you align your time, and what energy you share and connect with each day is a commitment to yourself, your whispers, and your frequency.

Even today, the house is not vacuumed, the dishes are in the sink and on the counters, I have no idea what we are eating for dinner, and the towels are not getting folded. Choosing me takes discipline and, at times, inconveniences other people, which I hate doing, as I want to be helpful and dependable. But, I have had to learn that time is one of your greatest gifts and I have to be mindful and purposeful about how I use and fill it.

Some people want everything in order before they start, which may clear your space and your head. Others want to be sure that the people around them have what they need before they make the time for a passion project. Only you can know how you show up and what you prioritize.

If you rarely get to the work that excites you, it might be helpful to monitor your actions and tasks each day to see where you are spending your time. *The Power of No* chart can also provide insight into what you are continuing to make time for. Knowledge is power, and getting honest about how you are spending your time can ensure it isn't slipping away from you, too.

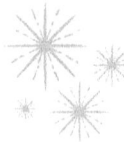

Key Finding #68

Only you can make the time for your life's work.

What can you let go of to make time for what you want to do?

_____

_____

Who is likely to beat you up the most about letting these things go?

_____

_____

Are you going to sidestep your whispers for this person? Even if it's your ego?

_____

_____

Most women do not see their life's work as work, as the skills required for our work are often aligned with talents that are uniquely our own, which is why our life's work requires us to prioritize ourselves from the inside out.

Key Finding #69

Honor your callings, embrace your seasons, and prioritize your whispers.

CHAPTER 48

BREAKING AWAY FROM PERFECTIONISM

I meet hundreds of women through my work who are ready for their next level of impact, yet they sit on the edge, contemplating if they are "ready enough." Like me, these women evaluate every potential outcome and frequently focus on the not-so-positive scenarios. With this lens, often filled with negative self-talk, they override their inner knowing and convince themselves that now is not the time. So, they wait.

Looking back, I now see that some of my self-imposed delays were dripping with doubt and unrealistic expectations. I often pressured myself to make others happy or avoided my fears of failure or embarrassment. Even on projects where I had little or no experience, I put enormous pressure on myself to create fantastic results. These ridiculous, self-imposed expectations kept me working nights and weekends, striving to be overprepared for the next opportunity.

Through my research for my second book, I learned that I was not alone. In the workplace, women often wait to be 100 percent prepared to apply for jobs, as opposed to men, who feel comfortable at around 60 percent prepared, according to Tara Sophia Mohr, author of *Why Women Don't Apply for Jobs Unless They're 100% Qualified*. Let's ask ourselves, how often do we require ourselves to be 100 percent ready or more for new things?

How have you held yourself back during the past two years because you were not 100 percent prepared?

_____

_____

What fears have you identified in previous chapters that you now realize have a STRONG hold on you and your aspirations?

_____

_____

What steps could you take this month to push through your self-doubts?

_____

_____

I met Faith while I was in New Orleans as a speaker for a women's event. Her email below provides great insight into these key findings:

Thank you for your presentation today. It resonated with me and I found it extremely valuable.

The difference in confidence levels between men and women in the workplace you spoke about is something I've been observing most of my life, both inside and outside of the work environment. Extremely competent women often express doubt with every mention of their accomplishments, while men are more likely to tout almost any accomplishment as a success and evidence of their value. Where that comes from is certainly the topic of many books, a few of which I've read. What is fascinating to me is how pervasive and consistent this gap is, considering the vastly differing experiences we've all had from each other in both adulthood and childhood. I see this reality from my seat as a manager in a tech company, to my seat in a bar next to men who are talking about cutting down trees.

You helped me form a connection, which you've likely already made, but I wanted to share with you. Unfortunately, the ways in which women sometimes show up at work based on the cultural values and behaviors we've been taught (many of which are fine and noble) have often been viewed as a weakness in a male-dominated workplace, which I now more clearly see is part of the reason women are statistically less likely to come into a conversation or opportunity without feeling 100% prepared. Many women have been chastised or ignored for not showing up in the same way as men or chastised and ignored for attempting to do so.

It was great to hear this dynamic discussed in a proactive, "What can we do to make our team stronger by learning to work with these differences?" way, rather than a "What's wrong with women at work?" way, as it so often is.

Thanks again,

Faith

What comes forward for you after reading this email?

_____

_____

Yes, I felt this delta of energy at work fueled by my need to fit in and prove I belong. With this, I used to think it was a compliment when people described me as a perfectionist, as it was a way of acknowledging that I was working hard to contribute in a meaningful way. Yet, after years of personal development, I now see perfectionism as more about wanting to fit in and working to avoid criticism or negative comments from peers, leaders, and co-workers.

I will let you know right now that it's not easy to break away from perfectionism, even though I recognized its grip on my life years ago and have worked to overcome it through self-development, spiritual alignment, and mind mapping.

I now realize that perfectionism is a trap that prevents us from digging deep, releasing guilt, and realizing that we do not need to seek external approval for self-worth. But even knowing this, I still see it trying to creep into my life every day.

Now when I was in the throes of perfectionism, I would have read the previous paragraphs and thought, *This author is missing the mark. I am not looking for acceptance from others or sidestepping criticism. I am doing more than is asked, all the time, because I want to get to the next step in my career goals.*

Let me ask you, what are you sacrificing to be a perfectionist?

_____

_____

How do you use perfectionism as an excuse in other areas of your life?

_____

_____

How have you sidestepped your well-being or wellness to meet your expectations of perfectionism?

_____

_____

For me, after reading dozens of books and receiving many energy sessions, I can now be candid. Going above and beyond is often a tool we use to convince other people and ourselves that we belong and are worthy of being here. The mind chatter or inner critic telling us we are not being good enough is fueled by, guess who? Our egos!

My perfectionism was always present but often in high gear when starting something new—the "something new" kickstarts my need to do it perfectly. But as we know, that is impossible because if we're doing something for the first time, we don't have that experience. So mistakes and missteps are inevitable, which should not impact our decision to start, try, or check out something new and definitely not make us second guess our likeability or self-worth.

Is there a particular project you were working on, a group of people you were trying to impress, or a particular time in your life when you believed perfectionism felt necessary?

_____

_____

Can you recall the first time you felt the need to get everything correct or even perfect?

_____

_____

When were you heavily praised for thinking of everything or doing the steps others forgot?

_____

_____

How has perfectionism impacted some of your whispers?

_____

_____

The concept of bringing professional women together to learn, connect, and share in nature came to me years ago as an inviting idea, as most of my events were held in offices or conference centers. My whispers and visions for these gatherings were vivid. However, the fear of failure and the fear of looking foolish absorbed my visions. Then layering the negative self-talk of not knowing exactly how to bring women together in this way, and the upfront investment, kept me in a holding pattern for years.

We could talk about our careers, but my whispers encouraged me to expand the conversation beyond work and family, with a desire to discuss our gifts, our exchange of energies, and our work here on Earth. I yearned to know what was hidden behind many women's titles, online profiles, and social activities.

Still loving my new nine-to-five work as a speaker and workshop facilitator, I could not shake this vision. I kept busy meeting women, enjoying the travel, and looking for signs. One hot summer afternoon, I was crammed into a bus moving from the Denver airport to a rental car lot. I felt sticky and was eager to get off because body odor was making its rounds. Even with these distractions, I decided to test myself to attempt to be fully present, drawing on my years of mindfulness training.

I felt my mind start to wander, and I brought it back to enjoying the view of the mountains. As I was admiring the landscape, the thought of contacting Dora appeared again and again. She is a spiritual guide who used a deck of playing cards to help me, and likely many others, align with my knowing. My mind jumped to *Maybe she can help me sort out these visions of bringing professional women together with an overnight retreat in nature.* I questioned my thoughts for a minute and even doubted she could help, but I decided to act on it immediately and sent her a text.

Now I know my mindfulness teacher, Suzanne Rusnak, would not be happy. I should have let that thought move right along, as mindfulness involves allowing thoughts to come and go without holding on to any one thought. But the thought was so unexpected, and the idea brought me so much excitement, that I jumped into action.

Within a week, Dora and I were on a call. Since we had talked before, I jumped right in. I provided an overview of current events in my life, focusing on this energy-based gathering for professional women that continued to appear in my thoughts But, I quickly added all the doubts and fears I was experiencing that had me at a standstill. Before I could finish, she interrupted me and forcefully asked, "What are you waiting for?"

"I'm not sure what to create."

She said, "Plan what you would want to go to!"

"Build what I want to go to?" I echoed back to her.

She said without a second to spare, "Yes!"

I sat there for a few minutes and tried to process her words.

"I am afraid," I blurted out.

"Afraid of what?" she asked with a supportive tone

"Failing…" I meekly shared.

"By whose standards?"

And then I was quiet. I did not know, as I didn't know anyone who was already hosting these types of overnight events for professional women. I had no one to follow and I had nothing, really, to compare it to. So what was overshadowing my vision? My fear was being served up by my ego, as this was something new.

As my mind was working through our quick-paced exchange, I heard Dora's voice again share, "JJ, build an overnight experience for women that you want to go to."

With mixed emotions, I could feel a tear roll down my face. *Is it that simple?* I wondered. *Build what I want to go to?*

Just as I felt a moment of inner peace, my engine of negative thoughts kicked in and started bombarding me with all the reasons it was not going to work. Then I realized I had once again prioritized external metrics, my fears, and peer approval.

Years after visiting Sedona, I still had to be aware of my ego, how it peppered my thoughts, and how it used fear as a tool to keep me dormant. Luckily for us, the Universe continues to deliver our teachers and lessons through different scenarios and situations.

I was grateful for Dora's time and direct message. It took me a few days to absorb, as I was unsure I could give myself permission. But her words eventually released my mental shackles. These shackles were filled with a need to deliver a perfect retreat that met every registrant's needs and expectations, which was ridiculous, as I had no experience creating an overnight retreat. My expectations of myself and my actions were preposterous, keeping me at a standstill for years.

Can you relate?

Can you think of a time when your expectations exceeded your experience and left you at a standstill?

_____

_____

Even with so much self-doubt, I decided to face my fears and move forward. I picked a date and focused on an agenda that excited me, including the Lightworkers and Energy Practitioners I was planning to invite based on individual sessions I had with each of them. The freedom to create an experience for the women was so exhilarating. Even though my ego continued to create self-doubt, I was determined to figure out the many unknown steps for this twenty-four-hour event.

As I moved through my thought processes, I asked myself, "What is the worst thing that could happen?"

I quickly responded, "No one registers."

This thought used to fill me with waves of fear about failing and being embarrassed, but this time I turned it around: *The worst thing that could happen is I would have a spiritual day for me.*

Suddenly, I viewed my starting point as an investment in myself rather than potential humiliation and a loss of funds. This was a huge money step for me, too, as losing money would previously have been a no-go situation. Now I see that the money I would use to create such an event is how I would want to spend my money even if no one attended, as the intention I had when creating the event was to embrace and celebrate the feminine energy on the planet.

I reencountered a similar message in Jen Sincero's *You Are A Badass*. She tells herself, "Let's just see what I can do." This statement, "Let me see," gives permission to check it out without expectations. What freedom, what possibilities emerge when we remove the expectations!

Is there something that continues to appear to you that you are waiting to launch?

_____

_____

What type of advice would help you move forward?

_____

_____

Can you restate your fears into opportunities to check out your ideas?

_____

_____

What can you do this month to see what is possible, even if you are not 100 percent ready?

_____

_____

For a lot of us, perfectionism started decades ago. For some, it stems from fear of not being good enough; others yearn for acknowledgment; and some seek acceptance. These stories have to go because now is not the time to hold yourself back. Even if you get a few nos, you are as prepared as you need to be right now to get moving in your desired direction.

As I mentioned before, I am not a big advocate for giant leaps out of the gate. I prefer reasonable and purposeful actions when approaching new endeavors. That being said, you decide what works for you.

Here are a few episodes from my podcast *Career Strategies for Women that Work* that can provide some additional insights on this topic with action-based strategies:

- Episode 3: Leaping from Impostor Syndrome to More Self-Efficacy [https://jjdigeronimo.com/3]
- Episode 9: Sidestepping Self-Doubt *Includes Fear Chart* [https://jjdigeronimo.com/9]
- Episode 15: 5 Wins from Every No [https://jjdigeronimo.com/15]
- Episode 17: Perfectionism is a Trap [https://jjdigeronimo.com/17]
- Episode 21: What Stories are Holding You Back? [https://jjdigeronimo.com/21]
- Episode 23: What Should You STOP Doing to START Thriving? [https://jjdigeronimo.com/23]
- Episode 33: Powerful Words – 5 Shifts to Harness Your Power [https://jjdigeronimo.com/33]

I have struggled most of my life with perfectionism—out of fear of not being good enough. Yet, over the past five years, I have leaped into new things without the intense desire to be perfect at them. In the past, I would have had second-guessed myself and likely sacrificed things that are important to me to go above and beyond, out of fear of not delivering my best. This intense pressure created anxiety and bad behaviors, but now, I accept and embrace that I am doing things for the first time and that I will make mistakes and likely miss the mark on some of my decisions.

With the help of great authors, guides and practices, I have worked to sidestep my self-doubts to step forward in my seeking. Now, I embrace the experience, cherish the opportunity, and recognize that it is the journey, as many say, and not the destination.

If you have been waiting, thinking, deciding, looking for approval, saving up your money, hoping it will work out, I encourage you to do one thing today to step in that direction. It could be as simple as a web search, phone call, registration, or commitment to yourself that now is the time.

As I was rounding out the last chapters of this book, I sent a few of the chapters to women in my network for an initial review. I was nervous but eager to get their initial feedback. Much to my surprise, one woman responded with, "I finally signed up." She did not share what it was, but my heart burst into joy!

It does not matter what or how, but it does matter when! When will you make time for your whispers?

 ### *Key Finding #70*

Perfectionism is a trap that holds our whispers captive.

CHAPTER 49

A RETREAT BEYOND
MY VISION

Weeks after my call with Dora, whom you can find on YouTube under the name AngelsLightTarot, in early 2018, I outlined my first Together We Seek retreat for women. I loved the name because I, too, was seeking alongside the women attending. There was no retreat leader per se, as we all were teachers, learners, and explorers coming together to pursue our truth and guidance.

With a setting in Mother Nature, nourishing meals, ancient practices, and meaningful conversations, I was excited to assemble a gathering for busy women to get them out of their schedules and traditional meeting spaces. My vision was based on what I thought I needed to reinvest in myself.

I extended the retreat invitation to women within my professional networks. This invite did not lead with my career-based topics, such as career advancement, positioning for a board seat, or leadership strategies. This invite was different, as it encouraged women to come together for twenty-four hours to explore mindfulness and energy practices that would help us slow down, connect with nature, and strengthen our connection with ourselves and other women.

Most of the women who registered for my retreat had attended at least one business conference that year and likely several throughout their careers. Their work weeks often included dinners and catered lunches.

With this gathering, I wanted to create a more nurturing experience. I chose to host this retreat at two houses in Vermilion, Ohio, on Lake Erie, rather than at a hotel. I love being by the water and I grew up going to this lake in Hamburg, New York, just South of Buffalo.

When envisioning this gathering, I felt compelled to create a space where women could come together within an intimate setting to focus on self-care and alignment. So, I hired Kathleen Madden, a fantastic organic chef who was so kind to trust and join me with this retreat, which was over an hour drive from her restaurant.

With her focus on local produce and farm-to-table experiences, I could think of no other to join us in Mother Nature. Nourishing our Souls through our bodies was one of the instrumental underpinnings of this gathering.

I would have liked to share that my fears were behind me, but as I prepared for the women to arrive, so did my fears. I experienced wicked cases of negative mind chatter, with a list of thoughts of all the things that could go wrong.

My inner work taught me that I had to get out of my head and move to my heart. With a desire to quickly shift this energy, I placed two fingers on the center of my forehead. Feeling the sensation of my fingers on my skin brought me back into the current moment.

If you are in a safe place where you can periodically close your eyes, you can work along with me as I describe how I shifted my self-doubting energy at that moment.

With my two fingers touching my forehead, I can feel the energy flow from my fingers down my body, through my feet, and into the ground. This is a quick exercise you can use at any time to clear and ground your energy.

For big influxes of energy, like I was feeling that day, you may need to do this a few times—visualizing the unwanted energy moving down your body, right into the ground.

Now that I was present and could feel the flow of energy from my fingers to my toes, I slowly moved my fingers down my forehead to the tip of my nose, dropped down to my lips, then pulled my fingers over my chin and down to my throat and neck. In less than thirty seconds, my fingers landed on my heart. I was pulling that negative energy down to my heart to engulf it with acceptance and love.

I felt immediate relief. My head seemed more open and my heart more spacious. It helped that I had practiced this for years, enabling me to shift my thoughts and energy from fear into gratitude in less than a minute. I allowed the neutralized negative energy to continue past my heart, down my body, and right into the ground.

Moving the energy around my body to create collaboration and alignment reminds me that I am part of a magnificent Universe that provides me with the inner peace that can wash away my expectations and fears.

On this wet spring day, the women started to arrive. Numerous times throughout the first hour, my mind chatter also arrived with silly thoughts like, *They think the house is too small*, and *This is not what they expected*, and *They think I charged too much*.

When I noticed these thoughts, I quickly tapped my toes or snapped my fingers. While these small physical actions were rarely noticed by others, they could get the attention of my mind so I could derail the freight train of fear-based thoughts. This gave me a chance to shift into a gratitude mindset, such as *What a blessing to have this amazing opportunity* and *How lucky am I to share this time with all these women?!*

After most of the women had arrived, I felt centered and ready for this new experience. The excitement among the women was overwhelming, and all the food Kathleen created was delicious and wholesome.

Even though I did not know all the women on a personal level, my intuition was right on. Our time together included great conversations, interactions, and energy-based sessions that were led by some of my favorite Lightworkers.

- Peggy Koelliker, an accountant by training and now a holistic energy coach and an Eden Energy Medicine practitioner.

- Carol Marchione, a Java developer and now certified Sound Healing & Energy practitioner.
- Sharon Ashcraft, a lifestyle educator, holistic medical advisor, and naturopath.

Although many of the practices were new to the women at this retreat, they seemed to enjoy these experiences, connections, and gifts from each other. I received many notes after the gathering, and I think Nicole's note sums it up perfectly:

I wanted to follow up and say thank you again for inviting me to your retreat.

Before the event, I mentioned I felt like I was in a rut. I think I can be really hard on myself. Especially when I am doing what I think is "the right thing to do" but I'm not seeing the results that I want yet—both personally and professionally. But after hearing the feedback from you and the group of women, I got the positive energy that I needed to get back at it. Although I am trying to wean myself off of external validation—it's just nice to hear it sometimes—especially from people that I admire. Again, thank you so much for such a fun experience! I am going to connect with everyone on LinkedIn soon as well!

Nicole

I did not fully anticipate the relationships, connections, and reciprocation that would blossom at these gatherings and carry on well after we said our goodbyes that weekend. Women connected and enriched each other's lives and journeys during our time together and beyond, which I often reflected upon after we departed.

In recent retreats, I have included ancient drumming, fire releases on the beach, tapping, iridology, essential oils, and Tibetan Singing Bowls with yoga. The amazing Energy Practitioners are all around us and often excited to join us, and the women who arrive as strangers leave feeling connected.

The beauty of these gatherings extends far beyond any of the expectations I had when I was sharing my vision with Dora. Had I known, I would have not let over three years slip away, which was about how long I sat on the vision. I was unsure what to do first or second and convinced myself that I was not ready, which was true, but the question becomes: When are we ever ready to do something new?

By stepping into my God-given gifts, I created a space for women to tap into other areas of wisdom and insight without shame or embarrassment. These safe opportunities empowered us to take more time for ourselves, especially in ways that encouraged us to become more refreshed, energized, and inspired.

Key Finding #71

Give your vision a chance to show you what is possible.

.

CHAPTER 50

LET YOUR WORK UNFOLD

Had I known that my adopted mindfulness practices and spiritual awakening would eventually lead me to host professional women's retreats and energy-based gatherings for women seeking, I am not sure I would have believed it. I am so energized by the connections and awakenings that occur among us.

During these gatherings, many share their current challenges and journeys that brought them to me. Several of the newcomers reveal how they never attended an overnight retreat and how they, too, felt guilty spending money on themselves for self-development, which reminded me of my "Ask" for my Sedona trip.

Many women have attended multiple *Together We Seek* retreats and brought along or recommended other women, which is a huge dose of awesomeness! It is hard to believe I second-guessed myself or waited years to launch. With glowing reviews from the women who attended and an undeniable inner peace from these gatherings, I am often planning the next retreat. With this, the Universe has graciously presented an amazing new gathering space filled with healing energy on the shores of Lake Erie in Vermilion, Ohio.

When I reflect on the nine years since I visited Sedona, I see how my life has expanded in many ways. With numerous lessons, I must remind myself that we all must step into our knowing. With the many demands of our lives, it can be challenging to step around our doubts, make time to visit our fuel stations, and prioritize work from the inside out, but it is essential. In addition to this, I work daily to let go of the guilt that creeps up on me and the external metrics that my ego continues to throw around in my head that try to define me.

After years of working off the side of my desk, I accepted more invitations to meet with women through organized events. My work takes me all over the world to gatherings of women that desire to have more impact and influence. Little did I realize that I, too, yearned for a deeper connection and impact. Afraid my idea would fail, I sat on it until Dora's words pushed me into action.

Her simple yet practical advice moved me from a place of fear to a place of action! "JJ, do what you love. Build a retreat you want to attend with an agenda you would want to invest in." I now see that creating more space for light in my life empowered me to be more open to the messages!

What messages, whispers, or nudges still come your way?

_____

_____

What is coming forward for you right now?

_____

_____

Are you at a frequency that attracts similar energy?

_____

_____

Is there a person, an action, or an activity calling you?

_____

_____

What things do you need to maintain in your schedule to cultivate nourishing energy for your whispers?

_____

_____

What tools will you explore or adopt to ease your ego-based thoughts and fears?

_____

_____

What adventure is calling you to kick-start your next chapter of seeking?

_____

_____

How will you create the space this month to align with your whispers?

_____

_____

I now know, after years of self-exploration, that my life's work as a human is to manage my frequency and brighten my light, which are both tested each day.

With my desire to continue my seeking, I was called to learn how my birth chart could shed light on my life's work. Your birth chart is also known as your astrology chart, which is the location of the planets at your time of birth.

During the pandemic, I signed up for two astrology courses—one with Molly C. Gauthier, and the other with Natalie Walstein, the creator of Soulshine Astrology—so I, too, could dive into the messages that the planetary placements provided for me. Our astrology charts, created by our birthdates with the exact times of our arrival, along with the locations of our births, can shine light on how we move along our journeys.

I loved this insight so much that I wanted to learn and share it. After two years of training, I gained additional wisdom on my life journey, my expected hurdles, and my gifts. Now, I create birth charts for my friends, family, and women in my network to help them identify obstacles and opportunities in their work and life.

Converting ancient wisdom into practical advice for women is so inspiring. With this additional level of insight, women utilize this information as they align with their work, lessons, and experiences.

With my Sun in the eighth house, it is no surprise that I like to dive into deep-seated topics that are not commonly discussed in public settings. Yet with my Chiron in my tenth house, I tend to feel self-conscious about my work, and at times uncomfortably vulnerable. I had a lot of fear talking about the topics I share here as part of my professional work; I was afraid people would think I was crazy, or not hire me because I talk about energy, or shame me at work events and conference tables if I included my insights from Lightworkers and energy practices.

I have recently experienced a Chiron return, which means it has traveled around all twelve signs of the zodiac wheel. This usually occurs near a person's fiftieth birthday. Chiron appears in different locations on our birth charts, which creates different lessons for each of us. When we help others with similar wounds, according to Greek mythology, then our Chiron return offers us the greatest rewards. This includes breaking through our fears and truly stepping into the work we agreed to do before we came down to the planet. With this, we can find beauty in our imperfections and trust our choices if we are aligning with love and light.

Off the side of my desk, I love sharing birth charts with women. I think they are a wonderful tool for additional insights into our lives and work. Finding new areas of guidance and inspiration often acts as a fuel station for me.

I see this experience of being here with you, right here, right now, as one of my life tests. A test to share my entire journey and not just what society deems to be an appropriate work conversation about the tools and strategies I used to push through my fears, self-imposed boundaries, and self-doubts. Many of these practices and tools I shared are still not deemed "acceptable," due to prevailing societal and religious norms.

This inside work and its accompanying self-exploration, with the help of energy practices and Lightworkers, have expanded my professional work and career to include *Together We Seek* retreats and an online community. This work will hopefully create a bridge for more women, and maybe men too, to learn, connect, and seek new levels of insight and self-awareness outside the usual paths.

Rest assured, you are on the right path, and being here with me now is no accident. As you have likely seen many times throughout these pages and through your answers to the many questions, each of us is on an individualized journey.

The great news is that we already have the wisdom and toolkit to make it our reality. No need to be alarmed; you already agreed to this work and have what it takes to align when you are ready. You may have to sharpen your offerings, but your knowing arrived with you and is buried in your Soul. There is no better time to sidestep your ego to let the work of your Soul shine.

This work requires us to dust off some gifts, sidestep some doubts, and realign the energy of our fears, but if I could push through my fears to share my journey and key findings right here in this book for all to see, read, and share, then I know you can, too.

I hope you found comfort in my stories and strength in my key findings. To balance the masculine energy of the planet, the world needs more women at more tables to infuse more feminine energy and their truth, wisdom, and gifts into more discussions, decisions, laws, leadership, solutions, and offerings.

With perspective and personal growth, I am an active believer in a Universal connection among all of us, providing numerous opportunities for us to help each other learn, grow, and awaken. For some of us, there is benefit in coming together, finding the space, and believing we are worth the time to explore our gifts to illuminate our paths.

This work empowers me, and hopefully you, too, to be more accepting, loving, and open to all the messages you receive. Bless your journey here and the work you are here to do.

 ### *Key Finding #72*

Shift your thoughts, align your actions, illuminate your life's work.

CHAPTER 51

LIGHT UP YOUR FREQUENCY

I am not suggesting my path should be your path. I love Jay from *Aquarian Insight's* advice, "Do not give up your power to anything or anyone." I do, however, encourage you to move toward what is calling you, even if you have some nerves around it. Trust your inner self and the wisdom you were born with as you tap into your knowing.

I am honored that so many Lightworkers, Energy Practitioners, Healers, and Carriers of Ancient Wisdom have crossed my path. Some of them offered new levels of awareness or assistance to remove unwanted energies, and others helped me level-up my intention to increase my energy, or, as I prefer to put it, raise my frequency.

Many have come through trusted sources and vetted paths. For example, during an acupuncturist session with Linda Corlett, I asked her about her favorite practitioners. She shared a few people and related experiences, which is how I learned about Dora and her gifts. Before I left that appointment, Linda happily handed me Dora's contact information.

With a new level of awareness and presence, I notice that little things each day appear before me, such as book titles, people, and event invitations. I encourage you to love yourself enough to do the work of self-discovery so that you can release and embrace your inner light. With this, do your research, ask people you love, and be your own advocate. If something feels off or not right, honor your light and remove yourself from the situation. For example, if you enter a space or group and get a weird vibe, do not stay because you would feel guilty leaving or changing your mind or because you may hurt another person's feelings. Be true to yourself, trust your whispers, and push through your self-doubt!

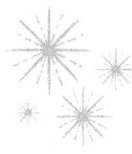

Key Finding # 73

Honor yourself, your light, and your knowing!

CHAPTER 52

FROM YOUR DESK

If you are looking to jump in, yet you are second-guessing your next action, your gifts, and your work, there is more beyond this book. It is hard to believe in things you have not explored or created in this lifetime, but you can start seeking off the side of your desk with just a few hours a week.

Showing up in the world each week, working inside yourself or toward things that light you up, lets the Universe know that you are ready to step into the next level of your life's work. Be sure to practice being present, mindful, and aware of all your actions, interactions, and synchronicities, as there are clues, opportunities, and gifts all around us.

Yes, there will likely be challenges and tears, but your gifts are special, and your work is sacred. Remember, your journey is all your own, and you will raise your frequency and align with more of your life's work if you create space to line up with your Universal light within. This is your time, and the resources, people, and momentum will appear as needed and when you are ready, so be sure to be aware and present for their arrival.

As you now know, I have not done this alone. I worked with many, many, many Energy Practitioners, Lightworkers, and Healers beyond the ones mentioned in the pages of this book who have helped me uncover my truth and inspired me along the way.

These beautiful human beings are lighthouses, utilizing their gifts to illuminate the path for many, as they too have done their internal work. They are often all around us, yet finding them can sometimes be time-consuming, which is why I launched TogetherWeSeek.Online.

Off the side of your desk, you, too, can learn about different practices, modalities, and experiences inside the community. I have been working to interview many of the Lightworkers that have crossed my path to highlight their learning, gifts, and journeys so that you can connect with those who resonate with your seeking.

With meaningful conversations, inspirational thoughts, and enlightened practices you can raise your energy, sidestep your self-doubt, and align with your life's work. Additionally, if you have already been working with these beautiful souls, I would love to hear about your work and their gifts!

I believe women hold the wisdom to shift their energy from within that will eventually harmonize the masculine and feminine energy of the planet. I encourage you to share your journey within your circles and beyond, as your words, actions, and light can be the catalysts for more women to step out in new ways. We all have more wisdom, knowing, and light within us.

Listen to Your Whispers

Seek Your Truth

Illuminate Your Light

With all my seeking to date, I could not be more thrilled to be on this journey with you as we work together to unleash our gifts and our knowing. Doing the work is worth it, and there is no excuse to not start now. As you likely now know, our life's work starts within!

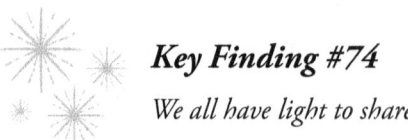 ### *Key Finding #74*
We all have light to share.

74 Key Findings is no accident!

After editing and restructuring this book, I was surprised to learn the deeper meanings behind the numbers from my friend and lightworker, Michele Laine,

Energetic Embodiment Coach and Master Quantum Numerologist. This is my interpretation of our conversation.

74 – The numbers 7 and 4 combined represent letting go of conditioning or patterns we have collected along the way that have been holding us back. This creates space for our light and gifts to shine through.

7 + 4 = 11 – The number 11 reminds us of our knowing and intuition with a powerful connection with the energies of the Universe, ourselves, and others.

1+1 = 2 – The spiritual number 2 highlights a partnership with the Universe, our inner self, and one another to work together to co-create, as you have a higher role on the Earth. My hope is this book gives you additional glimpses into your knowing that shape your journey ahead.

As you end this book, remember: You are one with all and you have everything you need, including support, love, wisdom, and connection to empower your whispers.

May you walk with the Winds

Align with the Rays

Flow with the Waves

And Shine for all to See

Bless your journey and the work you are here to do.

APPENDIX A: LIGHTWORKERS, URLS & WEBSITES

Introduction

Download: Questions from this book: https://jjdigeronimo.com/yourseeking

Community: Together We Seek: https://www.TogetherWeSeek.Online

6 - Summoned to Seek

Book: *The Working Woman's GPS: When the Plan to Have It All Has Led You Astray* by JJ DiGeronimo: https://jjdigeronimo.com/career-books-for-women

Book: *Accelerate Your Impact: Action-Based Strategies to Pave Your Professional Path* by JJ DiGeronimo: https://jjdigeronimo.com/career-books-for-women

9 – The "I Shoulds" of Success

Podcast: Episode 2: "Aligning Your Time and Actions with Your Goals," *Career Strategies for Women that Work*: https://jjdigeronimo.com/2

Course: The Power of No: https://jjdigeronimo.com/powerofno

11 – Internal Nudges

Book: *Accelerate your Impact: Action-Based Strategies to Accelerate Your Professional Path* by JJ DiGeronimo: https://jjdigeronimo.com/career-books-for-women/accelerate-your-impact

Website: Dr. Kinga Mnich: https://kingamnich.com

Video: Always/Whisper brand #LikeAGirl Campaign: https://www.youtube.com/watch?v=joRjb5WOmbM

12 – Follow the Whispers

Community: Tech Savvy Women LinkedIn© Group: https://www.linkedin.com/groups/124180

13 – Women Who Have Followed Their Whispers

Podcast: *Together We Seek*: https://podcasts.google.com/feed/
aHR0cHM6Ly9mZWVkcy5idXp6c3Byb3V0LmNvbS8xOTIzMDAxLnJzcw

Community: Envisioning Online Event 2022: https://www.togetherweseek.online/posts/
energy-practices-energy-boards-envision-the-2022-energy-you-desire

14 – Grounding Your Plan

Blog Post: "Nurture Your Flow Retreat ~ May 1, 2022," in Vermilion, Ohio: https://
jjdigeronimo.com/nurture-your-flow-retreat-may-1-2022

17 – Planning for a Solo Trip

Website: Rick at Sedona Soul Adventures: https://sedonasouladventures.com/befriending-
your-body-and-healing-yourself

Podcast: Episode #7: "Solo Trips – Creating Space for You," *Career Strategies for Women that
Work*: https://jjdigeronimo.com/podcast/episode-7-solo-trips-creating-space-for-you

18 – En Route to Sedona

Facebook Page: Stacey Alexander: https://www.facebook.com/stacey.alexander.777

Website: Omega Institute for Holistic Studies: https://www.eomega.org

Website: Kripalu Yoga and Wellness Center: http://kripaluyogaandwellnesscenter.org

Website: Sedona Soul Adventures: https://sedonasouladventures.com

Community: Share a fantastic guide or energy practitioner: www.TogetherWeSeek.Online

Website: Lily Dale: https://www.lilydaleassembly.org

TV Episode: "The Mediums of Lily Dale," *This Is Life With Lisa Ling*: https://tv.apple.com/
us/episode/the-mediums-of-lily-dale/umc.cmc.2nflos87lan989bwv4t10rgy5 or https://
www.imdb.com/title/tt9265808

20 – An Early Glimpse of My Life's Work

Website: Willow International: https://www.willowinternational.org

Article: "UN Women Take Action: 10 Ways You Can Help End Violence Against Women, Even During a Pandemic": https://www.unwomen.org/en/news/stories/2020/11/compilation-take-action-to-help-end-violence-against-women

Article: "You Suspect a Patient Is Being Abused. What Should You Do?": https://www.ama-assn.org/delivering-care/patient-support-advocacy/you-suspect-patient-being-abused-what-should-you-do

Website: Center for Domestic Peace: https://centerfordomesticpeace.org/tools-what-to-do-if-you-witness-abuse

21 – Seeds of Insight

Website: Bristol Hill Lavender Farm: https://www.bristolhillslavender.com

Blog Post: Susan's life and lavender journey: https://www.bristolhillslavender.com/1blog/1/10/2021

22 – Doubting Our Choices

Website: Super Soul Sunday: https://www.oprah.com/app/super-soul-sunday.html

Website: Lynne Twist: https://soulofmoney.org/

Podcast: "Lynne Twist: The Soul of Money" on *Oprah's Super Soul Conversations*: https://podcasts.apple.com/us/podcast/lynne-twist-the-soul-of-money/id1264843400?i=1000399867059

Book: *The Soul of Money: Transforming Your Relationship with Money and Life* by Lynne Twist: https://www.amazon.com/Soul-Money-Transforming-Your-Relationship/dp/0393353974

23 – Money Is the Hurdle for Many

Website: Suze Orman: http://www.suzeorman.com

Article: "40 Inspirational Suze Orman Quotes on Success": https://www.awakenthegreatnesswithin.com/40-inspirational-suze-orman-quotes-on-success

24 – Money – Abundance or Fear

Blog Post: "The Surprising Truth of Sufficiency" by Lynne Twist, posted on December 7, 2009: https://www.awakin.org/v2/read/view.php?tid=673

25 – Money Carries the Frequency We Give It

Book: *The Soul of Money: Transforming Your Relationship with Money and Life* by Lynne Twist: https://www.amazon.com/Soul-Money-Transforming-Your-Relationship/dp/0393353974

Book: *Get Rich, Lucky Bitch! Release Your Money Blocks and Live a First-Class Life* by Denise Duffield-Thomas: https://www.amazon.com/Get-Rich-Lucky-Bitch-First-Class/dp/1788171330/ref=tmm_pap_swatch_0?_encoding=UTF8&qid=&sr=

26 – Shifting into Abundance

Instagram Account: Beckett Johnson: https://www.instagram.com/spruceandsageco/ and https://www.instagram.com/tbithrivers

27 – Gratitude for Your Guides

Website: Malone Scholarship: https://www.jimmymalone.com

29 - Self-Worth Anchored in External Metrics

Wikipedia Page: "Sheryl Sandburg": https://en.wikipedia.org/wiki/Sheryl_Sandberg

Book: *Lean In: Women, Work, and the Will to Lead* by Sheryl Sadberg: https://leanin.org/book

30 – The Real Reason I Visited a Therapist

Wikipedia Page: "The Tower (Tarot card)": https://en.wikipedia.org/wiki/The_Tower_(Tarot_card)

Book: *The Seat of the Soul* by Gary Zukav: https://www.amazon.com/Seat-Soul-Gary-Zukav-1999-03-17/dp/B017V86WTG/ref=tmm_hrd_swatch_0?_encoding=UTF8&qid=&sr=

Interview: Mosaic's Magazine Interview with Gary Zukav and Linda Francis, July 9, 2008 – Issue 44, Fall 2008: https://mosaicmagazine.ca. This publication has since been retired.

Website: The Seat of the Soul Institute: https://seatofthesoul.com

Instagram Account: Alicia Thompson: https://www.instagram.com/aliciakimjoyful

Website: The Work of Byron Katie: https://thework.com

Community: Together We Seek: https://www.togetherweseek.online

31 – Did We Pick Our Mothers?

Website: Paula Marzaloes: http://www.paulamarzaloes.com

32 – Our Mothers Come with Soul Lessons

Website: Molly C. Gauthier: https://www.mollysastrology.com

33 – Releasing the Interdependencies

Website: Paula Marzaloes: http://www.paulamarzaloes.com

Book: *The Seat of The Soul* by Gary Zuvak: https://seatofthesoul.com/books

Wikipedia Page: "Heavenly Mother": https://en.wikipedia.org/wiki/Heavenly_Mother_
(Mormonism)

Facebook Page: Stacey Alexander: https://www.facebook.com/stacey.alexander.777

Wikipedia Page: "Archangel Michael": https://en.wikipedia.org/wiki/Michael_(archangel)

Community: Together We Seek: https://www.togetherweseek.online

34 – Recognizing the Energy Around You

Book: *The Seat of The Soul* by Gary Zuvak: https://seatofthesoul.com/books

Video: "Forgiveness Is Not What You Think—The Work of Byron Katie®":
https://www.youtube.com/watch?v=3mls5p1stcg

Website: Wendy Kimball: https://www.onebreathinstitute.com/wendy-kimball

35 – Our Relationships Mirror Our Energy

Podcast: "Past Life Regression – The Experience and Benefits with
Sarah Steel," *Together We Seek*: https://podcasts.google.com/feed/
aHR0cHM6Ly9mZWVkcy5idXp6c3Byb3V0LmNvbS8xOTIzMDAxLnJzcw/episode/
QnV6enNwcm91dC0xMDcyMTQ5Ng?sa=X&ved=0CAUQkfYCahcKEwiQm-
TM7Nr5AhUAAAAAHQAAAAAQAQ

Book: *The Universe Has Your Back: Transform Fear into Faith* by Gabrielle Bernstein: https://gabbybernstein.com/universe-has-your-back

Product Page: Oracle Cards: Kyle Gray's Keeper of the Light: https://www.amazon.com/gp/product/1781806969/ref=as_li_tl?camp=1789&creative=9325&creativeASIN=1781806969&ie=UTF8&linkCode=as2&linkId=0839a7821eb1ae75664778d-0c932417c&tag=kylegrayuk-20

Book: *Hidden Voices: Biblical Women and Our Christian Heritage* by Heidi Bright: https://www.amazon.com/Hidden-Voices-Biblical-Christian-Heritage/dp/1573121738

36 – Threads from Our Childhood Experiences

Website: Peggy Koelliker: https://www.healconnect.com

39 – Recognizing the Source of Your Energy

Wikipedia Page: "Jon Kabat-Zinn": https://en.wikipedia.org/wiki/Jon_Kabat-Zinn

Webpage: "About the Author," Jon Kabat-Zinn: https://www.mindfulnesscds.com/pages/about-the-author

Podcast: Episode 212: "The 7 Levels of Power" with Trenayce Talbert, *Awaken The Healing–Reclaim Your Life*: https://audioboom.com/posts/7773706-episode-212-the-7-levels-of-power

Podcast: Episode 221 "The 7 Levels of Power with Trenayce Talbert," *Awaken The Healing–Reclaim Your Life*: https://audioboom.com/posts/7902149-episode-221-lessons-unlearned

Website: Trenayce Talbert: https://www.awakenthehealing.com

Book: *Rising Strong: How the Ability to Reset Transforms the Way We Live, Love, Parent, and Lead* by Brené Brown: https://brenebrown.com/book/rising-strong

41 – Mindfulness and Meditation Intercept Self-Doubt

Website: Suzanne Cushwa Rusnak, MEd, MSSA, LSW, Cleveland Mindfulness: http://www.clevelandmindfulness.com

Wikipedia Page: "Jon Kabat-Zinn": https://en.wikipedia.org/wiki/Jon_Kabat-Zinn

Webpage: "About the Author," Jon Kabat-Zinn: https://www.mindfulnesscds.com/pages/about-the-author

Video Series: 10 Lessons I Gained From My Mindfulness Practice: https://www.jjdigeronimo.com/MindfulnessforWomen

44 – Lasso Your Energy

Wikipedia Page: "Chakras": https://en.wikipedia.org/wiki/Chakra

46 – Your Fuel Stations & Galactic Chips

Book: *You Are a Badass: How to Stop Doubting Your Greatness and Start Living an Awesome Life* by Jen Sincero: https://jensincero.com/shop

47 – Your Stories, Your Boundaries, and Your Seasons

Blog Post: Rebecca Campbell, "Rising and Falling and Falling and Rising": https://rebeccacampbell.me/the-reality-of-rising

Course: The Power of No: https://jjdigeronimo.com/powerofno

48 – Breaking Away from Perfectionism

HBR Article: Tara Sophia Mohr, "Why Women Don't Apply for Jobs Unless They're 100% Qualified": https://hbr.org/2014/08/why-women-dont-apply-for-jobs-unless-theyre-100-qualified

YouTube Channel: Dora ~AngelsLightTarot: https://youtube.com/c/AngelsLightTarot

Website: Suzanne Cushwa Rusnak, MEd, MSSA, LSW, Cleveland Mindfulness: http://www.clevelandmindfulness.com

Book: *You Are a Badass: How to Stop Doubting Your Greatness and Start Living an Awesome Life* by Jen Sincero: https://www.amazon.com/You-Are-Badass%C2%AE-Doubting-Greatness/dp/0762447699

Podcast: *Career Strategies for Women that Work*: https://jjdigeronimo.com/podcast

49 – A Retreat Beyond My Vision

YouTube Channel: Dora ~AngelsLightTarot: https://youtube.com/c/AngelsLightTarot

Website: Kathleen Madden, Chef: https://www.24kkitchen.com

Website: Peggy Koelliker, Holistic Energy Practitioner/Instructor and Professional Development Coach: https://www.healconnect.com/

LinkedIn Page: Carol Marchione, Sound Healing Practitioner & IT Consultant: https://www.linkedin.com/in/carol-marchione

Facebook Page: Sharon Ashcraft, Lifestyle Educator and Holistic and Naturopath Advisor: https://www.facebook.com/sharon.ashcraft1213

50 – Let Your Work Unfold

Website: Molly C. Gauthier, Experienced Astrologer and Holistic Health Coach Practitioner: https://www.mollygauthier.com

Website: Natalie Walstein, Career Astrologer: https://www.soulshineastrology.com

51 – Light Up Your Frequency

Website: Jay, Aquarian Insight: https://www.aquarianinsight.com

Website: Linda Corlett, Acupuncturist: https://www.facebook.com/profile.php?id=100071652363299

52 – From Your Desk

Website: Michele Laine, Energetic Embodiment Coach and Master Quantum Numerologist: http://www.michelelaine.com

APPENDIX B: TOGETHER WE SEEK PODCAST

Episode 1: "Spiritual Seeking – Maneuvering Family Traditions and Religious Practices," March 16, 2022

Episode 2: "Human Design – How to Use It for Your Work & Life + 5 Design Types," March 18, 2022

Episode 3: "Qi & Qigong Inside and Outside of Work with Samm Smeltzer," Mar 25, 2022

Episode 4: "Numerology – How Can It Provide Insight into Our Work & Life with Michele Laine," Apr 1, 2022

Episode 5: "What Are Birth Charts & How Can They Share Career Insights!," April 14, 2022

Episode 6: "Co-Create with the Universe & Strengthen Your Resilience with Dawna Jones," April 22, 2022

Episode 7: "Face Reader and Energy Medicine Practitioner Kathleen McManis," Apr 29, 2022

Episode 8: "Our Stories and Vulnerabilities with Certified Bryon Katie Coach Alicia Thompson," May 6, 2022

Episode 9: "Energetically Healing Our Past with Intensive Care Nurse of 41 Yrs Ruth M Kent," May 27, 2022

Episode 10: "Clearing Ancestral Energy with Jacqueline Kane," June 10, 2022

Episode 11: "The Inner Journey to Empowerment with Author Amy Edelstein," June 24, 2022

Episode 12: "Past Life Regression – The Experience and Benefits with Sarah Steel," July 8, 2022

Episode 13: "Why Start Your Own Retreats with Ella Lucas-Averett & JJ DiGeronimo," July 15, 2022

Episode 14: "What is Psych-K®" with Sue Begent," July 22, 2022

Episode 15: "Emotional Healing for Empowerment with Rita Carnevale," August 7, 2022

Episode 16: "Tapping into the Power of Your Menstrual Cycle – Dr. Kinga Mnich," August 26, 2022

Episode 17: "The Unexpected Journey to a Certified TRE® Provider with Wendy Kimball," September 9, 2022

Episode 18: "Harness the Power of Your Subconscious Mind with Mary Kacaba," September 23, 2022

Episode 19: "Spiritual Travel with Heidi Bright," October 7, 2022

Episode 20: "The Secret Wisdom of Playing Cards with Susie Gale," October 21, 2022

Find *Together We Seek* on popular podcast platforms:

Apple Podcast: https://podcasts.apple.com/hr/podcast/together-we-seek/id1618591942

Audible Podcast: https://www.audible.com/pd/Together-We-Seek-Podcast/B09XKJZLQW

Google Podcast: https://podcasts.google.com/feed/
aHR0cHM6Ly9mZWVkcy5idXp6c3Byb3V0LmNvbS8xOTIzMDAxLnJzcw

Spotify: https://open.spotify.com/show/
5YeYkzcHwmuQyFUFLAQOJK

APPENDIX C: GRATITUDE EXERCISE - ABUNDANCE PROMPTS

From **Chapter 25 – Money Carries the Frequency We Give It**

I'll bet you have more beautiful things happening each day than you realize. Noticing and listing out all the abundance and love that comes your way can create momentum for more love and abundance.

Day 1: This is how the Universe has sent me love and abundance today

1. _____
2. _____
3. _____
4. _____
5. _____
6. _____
7. _____
8. _____
9. _____
10. _____

Day 2: Look at the abundance the Universe has shared with me today

1. _____
2. _____
3. _____
4. _____
5. _____
6. _____
7. _____

8. _____

9. _____

10. _____

Day 3: Big and small, I can see how I am showered with love from the Universe

1. _____

2. _____

3. _____

4. _____

5. _____

6. _____

7. _____

8. _____

9. _____

10. _____

Day 4: I am seeing the synergies in my day and the love from the Universe

1. _____

2. _____

3. _____

4. _____

5. _____

6. _____

7. _____

8. _____

9. _____

10. _____

Day 5: I am surprised by how many little things the Universe sends my way each day

1. _____

2. _____

3. _____

4. _____

5. _____

6. _____

7. _____

8. _____

9. _____

10. _____

Day 6: I am seeing the focus shift right before me, as abundance is everywhere

1. _____

2. _____

3. _____

4. _____

5. _____

6. _____

7. _____

8. _____

9. _____

10. _____

Day 7: I am grateful that I have taken the time to log all that the Universe sends my way

1. _____

2. _____

3. _____

4. _____

5. _____

6. _____

7. _____

8. _____

9. _____

10. _____

Day 8: Lucky me—I am now more aware of my blessings

1. _____

2. _____

3. _____

4. _____

5. _____

6. _____

7. _____

8. _____

9. _____

10. _____

Day 9: What I focus on expands; the abundance is showing up in so many ways

1. _____

2. _____

3. _____

4. _____

5. _____

6. _____

7. _____

8. _____

9. _____

10. _____

Day 10: I am unique, beautiful, and full of the abundance I need to do my work

1. _____

2. _____

3. _____

4. _____

5. _____

6. _____

7. _____

8. _____

9. _____

10. _____

I am blessed. You are blessed, too, with abundance, love, and access to a frequency that will illuminate your path based on your gifts, knowing, and desires. As you collect your abundances each day, you can say your own prayer of gratitude or use mine:

"Thank you for the abundance in love, connections, experiences, and growth. I feel rich from the energy I create, share, and receive within my work and throughout life."

APPENDIX D: VISUALIZATION – GROUND RELATIONSHIP ENERGY

From **Chapter 35 – Our Relationships Mirror Our Energy**

When relationships or frequencies no longer align, the Universe does what it does best—ushering me along. With this, you may have some lingering energy associated with this shift.

I visualized a cleaning that started at the top of my head, moved down my neck and throat, down my chest and torso, and through my stomach, pelvis, and back. Then it went down my thighs, over my knees, through my calves, over my ankles, into my feet, down into the floor, and into the Earth. My friend, editor, and author of many books, including *Hidden Voices: Biblical Women and Our Christian Heritage*, Heidi Bright, shared that the darker energies get mulched by Mother Earth.

This resonates with me, as I then think of all the beautiful flowers that grow in mulch. This movement of energy flowing out of my body into Mother Earth creates energetic space throughout my body where the light can shine and illuminate my path for what is next.

As you spend time clearing out the stories, dependencies, and even darkness, the light will emerge, which may not be immediately apparent. But trust me, if you work to clear out the dark energy and align with more gratitude for the things in your life, you will eventually encounter new people and experiences that align with your upgraded frequency.

APPENDIX E: MINDFULNESS EXERCISE – GET PRESENT IN MINUTES

From **Chapter 42 – The Present of Mindfulness**

Find fifteen minutes in your schedule, a quiet space, and a comfortable seat. Bring a notebook or piece of paper with you. Set your timer for fifteen minutes. When you start the time, observe everything around your selected area and write down everything you experience.

Now fifteen minutes is a long time to be observing, so do not be surprised if you initially run out of things to write down. Remember, you can use all five senses as you take in your surroundings. This is a judgment-free space, so observe, log, and move on. If you find yourself adding comments to your observations, such as "I need to water that plant" or "That wall needs a new coat of paint," recognize that you have drifted into creating future tasks. Instead, focus on identifying and logging without letting your mind have an opinion or additional thoughts about the item listed. Feel free to revisit things you observe multiple times, recognizing other aspects or new interpretations. For example, if you logged a TV, consider capturing any reflection on the screen, or shift your awareness to what you hear. What sounds you are hearing around your space? Consider grouping some of your views. If you have a plant, how many leaves are pointing North?

Each time you practice being in the current moment, you will work to remind your ego that there is more to you than the mind chatter and stories it serves up on a regular basis. Being present takes time and practice, especially with an active mind that wants to be productive.

A mindfulness practice can help you recognize the non-stop chatter that many of us experience, distracting us from the present moment. One way to keep working on being in the present moment is to set your next observation time every time you end.

APPENDIX F: MINDFULNESS EXERCISE – SHIFTING NEGATIVE MIND CHATTER

From **Chapter 49 – A Retreat Beyond My Vision**

I placed two fingers on the center of my forehead to shift self-doubting energy. Feeling the sensation of my fingers on my skin brought me back into the current moment.

With my two fingers touching my forehead, I can feel the energy flow from my fingers down my body, through my feet, and into the ground. This is a quick exercise you can use at any time to clear and ground your energy.

For big influxes of energy, like I was feeling that day, you may need to do this a few times—visualizing the unwanted energy moving down your body, right into the ground.

Now that I was present and could feel the flow of energy from my fingers to my toes, I slowly moved my fingers down my forehead to the tip of my nose, dropped down to my lips, then pulled my fingers over my chin and down to my throat and neck. In less than thirty seconds, my fingers landed on my heart. I was pulling that negative energy down to my heart to engulf it with acceptance and love.

I felt immediate relief. My head seemed more open and my heart more spacious. It helped that I had practiced this for years, enabling me to shift my thoughts and energy from fear into gratitude in less than a minute. I allowed the neutralized negative energy to continue past my heart, down my body, and right into the ground.

Moving the energy around my body to create collaboration and alignment reminds me that I am part of a magnificent Universe that provides me with the inner peace that can wash away my expectations and fears.

Keep Seeking

www.ingramcontent.com/pod-product-compliance
Lightning Source LLC
Chambersburg PA
CBHW071142130626
46553CB00004B/1483